BEST PUB WALKS

in and around

CENTRAL LONDON

Ruth Herman

Published by Sigma Leisure – an imprint of
Sigma Press, 1 South Oak Lane, Wilmslow, Cheshire SK9 6AR, England.

British Library Cataloguing in Publication Data
A CIP record for this book is available from the British Library.

ISBN: 1-85058-427-3

Typesetting and Design by: Sigma Press, Wilmslow, Cheshire.

Cover illustration and cartoons: Martin Mills

Printing, maps and cover design: MFP Design & Print

Disclaimer: the information in this book is given in good faith and is believed to be correct at the time of publication. No responsibility is accepted by either the author or publisher for errors or omissions, or for any loss or injury howsoever caused. Only you can judge your own fitness, competence and experience.

Preface

There are many books on London, and there are quite a few about walks in London. There is also a fair-sized collection of books on pubs in London. All I have tried to do is to combine some of all these features into one volume, giving the reader an idea of routes which are interesting in themselves, but with the bonus of regular pub-stops on the way.

Most popular pubs these days are open all day from 11.00 am to 11.00 pm, so a walker should have no trouble from Monday to Saturday. There is a move afoot to abolish Sunday opening hours (at present pubs must close by law from 3.00 pm to 7.00 pm). I have only one word of warning - City of London pubs are often closed all weekend and from relatively early in the evening. Other than this, you should have no trouble obtaining refreshment from any of the pubs in this book.

I lay no claim to any startling new insights into London's history and in so far as I owe an incalculable debt to all those people who have written books on London before me, it goes without saying that if you have a serious interest in the history of this great metropolis, then you will already know that there are some very scholarly and entertaining books written. I have found several invaluable and I would strongly recommend *The London Encyclopaedia*, edited by Ben Weinreb and Christopher Hibbert.

Another great source of information (although requiring somewhat more stamina) is the six volumes of the Victorian *London Recollected* by Edward Walford. John Stow's *Survey of London* takes us back to the sixteenth century and is charming in its own right, as well as being a fund of information. If you have a taste for the seamier side of life, the title of E.J. Burford's *London: The Synfulle Citie* I think speaks for itself.

But there are also many, many books on specific areas of London. I suggest a visit to your local library will reveal that something has already been written on almost every nook and cranny of the place.

But whether you decide to read more or just want to browse through this little volume, of one thing I can be sure. You will end up quoting Dr Johnson: "When a man is tired of London, he is tired of life; for there is in London all that life can afford".

Ruth Herman

A Warning Note!

Even the most intrepid and daring Londoner is advised to carry a trusty "A-Z" map book while following these walks. It is too easy to take a wrong turning and become very lost in London. And in the most 'touristy' areas there is little point in asking a passer-by, because they're probably lost too!

So take my advice (borne of years of wandering the streets of our great capital city with little or no idea of what direction I'm going in) – don't leave home or hotel without a London street gazetteer.

On the other hand, there is no better way to discover some of the most delightful, interesting and curious parts of London than taking a wrong turning. But it's comforting to know where you should be and how to get back there!

However, neither I nor the publisher take any responsibility for shoe repairs necessitated by unauthorised wandering off my intended route, whether caused by my directions or the reader's interpretation of them.

Mind you, if you do find something really interesting, please let us know!

Contents

1. Westminster, Whitehall and The Strand

Highlights: Houses of Parliament, Whitehall, Downing Street, The Cenotaph, Trafalgar Square, Charing Cross, Savoy Hotel, Lyceum Theatre.

Stations: Westminster and Temple

Distance: 2¼ miles

London changes from one street to the next, but if there is one area which has seen a secure hold on power throughout the country, it must be Westminster and Whitehall. They are the traditional seats of government and have been for hundreds of years. The pubs along this route have been used to provide for civil servants and politicians, and there is a long tradition in this part of town of royalty, nobility, administrators and just plain hangers-on.

The Walk

Starting at Westminster Station, the first thing you will see is the Houses of Parliament, the pride of many a postcard home. It is also the home to the most famous clock in the world, Big Ben (which is either named after the very large Chief Commissioner of Works in 1857 or an equally-large Benjamin Caunt, an 18 stone prize-fighting publican of the Coach and Horses pub in St Martins Lane.) The buildings (as most people know by now) are, first of all, a Victorian extravaganza built to replace the original which burnt down in a huge fire of 1834. Some of you might find it comforting that the fire started legitimately enough as an attempt to burn hundreds of years of redundant financial records and ended up with the Mother of Parliaments as a pile of smoking ruins. Since then war time bombers also did a pretty effective job demolishing the House of Commons – so some of it is only as old as about 1950! Maybe they should have followed Victorian designer and author William Morris' suggestion that they turn the place into "dung market" – do I hear someone say "how can you tell the difference?" Since this walk isn't about politics, let's not be drawn into that discussion!

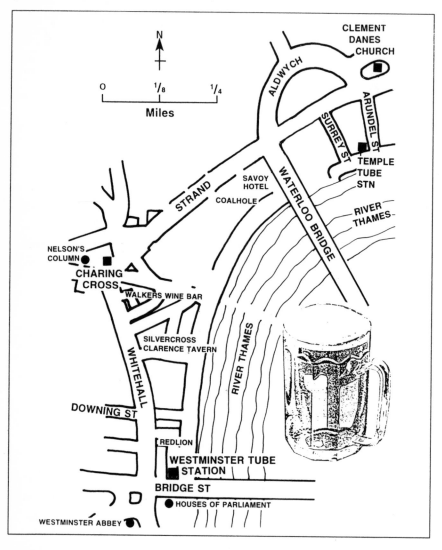

But let us leave Westminster. Cast an eye back to Westminster Bridge if you will and reflect on the freak shows that could be seen there in the late 1770s including a creature that seemed "to be a link between the Rational and Brute creation, as he is a striking resemblance of the Human Species" – but I said that we weren't going to talk about Members of Parliament!

Whitehall

We have to turn right as we come out of the station and walk down towards Parliament Street and then Whitehall. (Look at Whitehall – it is the widest street in London and several streets were demolished to provide sufficient space in the roads around it. It was obviously not before time, because there was at least one murder when tempers got a touch frayed in a traffic-jam induced brawl.) Here we turn right again and come to our first pub – The Red Lion.

The attractive, heavy Victorian exterior is matched by the heavy wooden panelling inside. The pub is remarkable for two things. Firstly, it is built on the site of the tavern into which David Copperfield goes on his twelfth birthday to have a lonely celebratory glass of "Genuine Stunning Ale". The landlady (in the novel) took pity on the poor little lad and gave him the beer free plus a motherly kiss. This story and the Dickens connection is commemorated in the fabric of the building with a bust of the author who looks down on passers-by.

You are unlikely to see a 12-year-old fictional hero in the pub these days and even less likely to be handed your ale with a kiss, but you are quite likely to see back-bench MPs eating one of the pub's excellent lunches in the upstairs restaurant or talking to the landlord. A Division Bell is installed in the building to call the elected representatives back to the House to vote. Rumour has it that bullet-proof glass has been installed and there is a small TV studio upstairs for journalists to record interviews. After leaving the Red Lion continue down Whitehall.

Downing Street

On the opposite side of the road to the pub, Downing Street is worthy of a glance through the railings if only to reflect on the lowly origins of one of the most famous addresses in the world. Built by the slippery Sir George Downing, at one time boss to Samuel Pepys, as well as becoming home to The First Lord of the Treasury (Prime Minister) it could also claim as residents James Boswell (Dr Johnson's biographer and lad-about-town) and Tobias Smollett the author. Boswell describes it as "a genteel street . . . and very healthful". He paid a mere 40 guineas per year and one shilling a time to dine with his landlord.

Early Prime Ministers turned their noses up at this comparatively humble residence and let it to junior colleagues. Can you see that happening nowadays?

Now continue past the Cenotaph (originally only intended as a temporary structure, but so popular that it was decided to make it into a permanent memorial) and then look down towards Trafalgar Square and see the line of statues to dead generals looking up towards the Cenotaph. Is it design or ironic chance that the men who ran the wars are forced to spend eternity looking at the memorial to the people who died in the wars?

It is also ironic that a statue to poor old Sir Walter Raleigh is here as well. Sir Walter, whose only fault (if there is any truth in the legend) was bringing tobacco into the country (though how could he have known how much damage he was doing – and anyway if it hadn't been him it would have been someone else!), spent many years as a prisoner in the Tower of London. He was finally beheaded by James I who particularly disliked tobacco, but I suspect it wasn't entirely the reason he had poor Sir Walter beheaded. Who knows, perhaps Sir Walter communicates with that other famous decapitee, King Charles I (the son of James I), whose statue stands just past the bottom of Whitehall, at Charing Cross. Charles sits on his horse looking up towards Parliament towards the statue of the man who had him beheaded, Oliver Cromwell. (But Charles had the last laugh because Parliament actually refused to pay for Oliver's statue, even though he was their most faithful champion!)

As you walk past Sir Walter you are very close to the spot where Charles was beheaded. Charles commissioned Rubens to paint the magnificent ceiling in the Banqueting Hall (which you will pass on the right past the Red Lion) where he spent his last few minutes on earth. Perhaps if this ill-fated monarch had stuck to buying paintings, the Roundheads and Cavaliers would never have crossed pikes.

Continue on further down Whitehall and The Clarence Tavern is a reminder that neither terrorism nor making a profit out of adversity is something that was invented in the past few years. The archway that used to connect the Clarence to its neighbouring building was blown up in the late nineteenth century by Irish Fenians. The damage was extensive, but the pub landlord paid for the removal of the irreparable arch by charging sightseers threepence per head and of course taking advantage of the thirst generated by enthusiastic sightseeing!

The Silver Cross Tavern is the next pub of interest. The first record of licensing for the tavern is for a Joseph Craig in 1674. Because of its proximity to what was once the Royal household in Whitehall Palace, the pub has to have its licence renewed each year at the Board of the Green Cloth. This archaic institution was formed in the fourteenth century to exercise control over the environs of the Royal family – they had to be protected, after all, from "brawling, drunkenness, thieving and so on". (The Silver Cross was, according to one source, also a well-known brothel so we have to suppose it was at least discreet in its activities – or else the convenience of having its "wares" on their doorstep was appreciated by the Palace. Whatever the case it has also been commented that the fineness of the ceiling was no doubt much a great comfort to the girls while they were at work!)

Curiously enough, even though their Majesties now live some way away, local pubs still have to go through the same licensing process. This I can understand – but when did you last hear of a riot within the venerable precincts of the Royal Society and the National Gallery? We are obviously missing out on something because they also have to be licensed by the Board!

Craig Court, next on our route, is notable not only for a very pleasant wine bar called Walker's but also for an amusing story about an eighteenth-century speaker of the House of Commons whose coach got firmly stuck in the alley. The poor man finally had to be pulled out through the roof! One could muse as to whether in a later age he would have had a fully comprehensive insurance policy with Sun Life, who were formed here as the Sun Fire Office in 1726.

Charing Cross

Now we go past Trafalgar Square, and continue down the Strand past Charing Cross and where the statue of Charles I now stands. While you walk past Charing Cross, reflect on its colourful history. In its time these few square yards have seen a monument to the dead Queen Eleanor, wife of Edward I, a fish shop, an execution block (ironically for the men who signed Charles I's death warrant), the first Punch and Judy Show to be seen in England, two pubs and a bank. Hardly any wonder that Dr Johnson commented that "the full tide of human existence is at Charing Cross"!

As you walk down the Strand look at the roads just behind it and note their names. String them together and you make "George Villiers, Duke Of Buckingham" – this was a result of the owner of the area in the 1670s insisting that before he sold the land he be remembered for ever in the place. "Of Alley" has become York Place but true to this early landowner's wish, the name is still preserved underneath the street sign. Buckingham Street has since been home to an extraordinary variety of famous names – Samuel Taylor Coleridge, Henry Fielding, Jean-Jacques Rousseau, Dickens and even the Russian Czar Peter the Great!

As we walk down the Strand we will eventually come to The Coal Hole, another extremely pleasant pub, well worth a visit. First I must point out that the Coal Hole that you see is not The Coal Hole which I am going to describe. That pub was originally a drinking place for the coal-heavers who plied their trade up the Thames and could call in at what was originally a pub not far from the river (the Embankment is relatively new and was built by the Victorians to hide the nasty sludgy banks of the river Thames). In the old pub they could enjoy such delights as stewed eels, cow-heel, tripe and onions, liver and bacon and sausages and mash (maybe some of which are still on the menu today).

Among the boasts of the original Coal Hole was that it was one home of the notorious early nineteenth-century actor Edmund Kean's disreputable Wolves Club who, it was said, were dedicated to protecting their founder and booing rival tragedians off the stage.

Whether or not that was their aim, they certainly had a reputation for unruly behaviour, drinking huge quantities of liquor and indulging in a great deal of raucous singing (perhaps the basis of the rumour that the Wolves Club was founded for men whose wives would not allow them to sing in the bath?!). Later on the singing got better and the pub became a convivial song-and-supper venue giving late-night revellers somewhere to go after the theatre. There is even a legend that Lord Byron once popped in for a drink after the theatre, but found the atmosphere "too merry" for his taste.

Another of the less charming amusements to be found in The Coal Hole in the 1850s was something called "The Judge and Jury Entertainments" which featured mock divorce trials which were as seedy and smutty as they thought they could get away with. It obviously appealed to the Victorians since during the first summer in 1851 (during the Great Exhibition) it was playing three times per night. Would mock divorce trials these days even begin to match the real thing?

The Savoy

The old pub was swept away when the Savoy Hotel was built on the land between 1889 and 1904 and the new pub took on the old name. But even this new pub has at least one good story attached to it – it was the haunt of the well-known creative drinker, the Welsh poet Dylan Thomas, who one night apparently got a real fright from the eccentric Aleister Crowley (known as The Great Beast and with a reputation for Devil Worship sinister enough to give anyone second thoughts about asking him what he was up to). Thomas who was idly doodling away noticed Crowley watching him from the other end of the bar. Eventually Crowley left and slipped Thomas a piece of paper. At first, the poet was too frightened to turn over the sheet but eventually when he did he saw that the "necromancer" had doodled precisely the same sketch as he had. Explain that if you can! Perhaps you should stick to the beer in the Coal Hole – we don't want to encourage any rash encounters with spirits here!

If you're feeling a little too grand (like Lord Byron) to go into the

Coal Hole, try the Savoy Hotel. It was in these grand premises that Peach Melba (named after the visiting Dame Nellie Melba, the opera singer) first saw the light of day; Ritz was the first hotel manager here and Escoffier was the first chef. Nothing but the best here!

Before we get to the (now closed) Aldwych Station, drop in for a last quick drink at the Lyceum Tavern which is around the corner from the Lyceum Theatre. Just beyond this site in Wellington Street, the Lyceum had been, among other things, a circus, the site of Madam Tussaud's first wax works exhibition in London and the first place where gas lighting was demonstrated in the capital. Samuel Beazley rebuilt it in 1816 on its present site and its history is even more chequered, although it did at one time boast Henry Irving as its principle actor. Beazley himself is commemorated in the pub (which has a special door in the bar to allow stage staff in) with the following immortal words:

"Here lies Samuel Beazley
Who lived hard and died easily"

Here we are at the end of the walk and ready to go home (although if you're a real glutton for pubs and walking, you could turn left up past the Lyceum and find yourself in Covent Garden!)

Alternatively, carry on along The Strand, turn right past the now-closed Aldwych Station, down Surrey Street and left at the bottom into Temple Place and you will be able to catch a train at Temple Station.

2. Hampstead and its Heath

Highlights: Golders Green, and its once-famous Hippodrome; Ivy House, the home of Anna Pavlova; Hampstead village, where the young set hang out; Hampstead pubs that have played host to hundreds of literary characters from Dickens to Thackeray.

Stations: Golders Green and Hampstead

Distance: 1½ miles

This must be one of the most pleasant walks you can do in suburban London. There cannot be an inch of Hampstead which has not been walked on by someone you've heard of. Even nowadays, you can still see familiar (or notorious) faces walking past you. Writers, politicians, and media folk (in fact anyone with money and/or intellectual aspirations) find a spell in this ruthlessly unspoilt neighbourhood does their career no harm. (As you might expect Hampstead is a breeding ground for pressure groups – no-one is sacrosanct. Even McDonalds had a hard time getting in here!) Very soon after you set out you will find yourself walking past trees, a fine "unspoilt" heath and some of the prettiest houses in London.

The Walk

We start out in relative anonymity. It has to be admitted that Golders Green is not the first place you would go to find famous faces. The place only dates from the beginning of this century! Before the railway arrived in 1905 the place was fields, farms and a few country houses. Turn left out of Golders Green Station on to North End Road and walk past the home of the BBC Concert Orchestra which used to be Golders Green Hippodrome (this is the biggest building in the area). Anna Pavlova, the famous ballerina gave her last public performance at the Hippodrome (which was very convenient since she lived just down the road as we shall see later!)

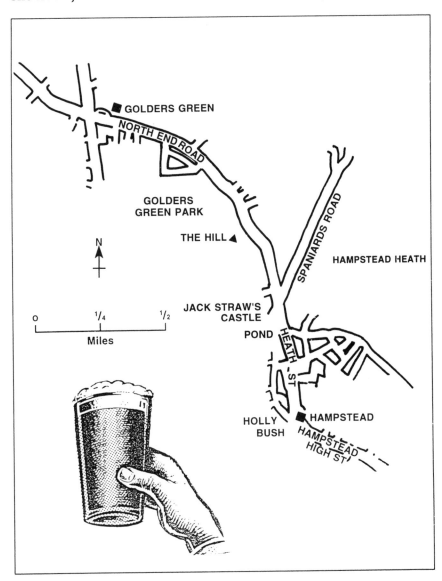

The road is full of spacious Edwardian houses, and even here we can see the first traces of the intellectual elite who have, for many years, graced Hampstead's pleasant roads. There is a blue plaque announcing that Evelyn Waugh used to live in one of these relatively unassuming Edwardian houses (he went to school just up the way, as again we shall see later). Perhaps it was here he dreamed of living in the kind of place featured in 'Brideshead Revisited'? Perhaps not. But it is opposite to a public park so maybe Waugh could pretend it was his country estate!

As we walk up the hill (the only climb we have on this walk) we come to increasing signs of affluence. King Alfred School is on the left – it is both progressive and expensive. And you will notice that the Headmaster from 1901 – 1920 was John Russsell.

Golders Hill

I don't know if there were swans in Golders Hill Park then, from which Pavlova could judge her own famous portrayal as The Dying Swan but these days, in the park's charming children's zoo, you are more likely to see rather inelegant ducks waddling past. On a summer's day this little park is worth a detour if only to allow ourself to quote the eighteenth-century poet Akenside:

"Thy verdant scenes O Goulder's Hill
With throbbing temples and with burden'd breast
Once more I climb thy steep aerial way
. . . Dissolve this rigid cough profound"

It seems to me that Akenside did not take my advice and probably walked this route the wrong way round! Wordsworth too claimed that he was "a not unfrequent visitor" past the gates to Golders Hill (although that was when it was part of a private house and not a municipal park!) Otherwise he could have listened to the Bandstand or played with the ducks – if he went in the spring it could even have been here he saw his "host of golden daffodils"! From here on in on this walk I would advise you to keep your pocket edition of a

Guide to English Literature close by you – because as you get nearer to Hampstead the poets and novelists get ever thicker on the ground (not only did they live here they visited each other all the time, so that, yes you guessed it, you're not safe from Dr Johnson or Dickens even in these northern reaches!) It has to be said somewhere (and why not here?) that if Dickens and Johnson spent so much of their lives enjoying themselves, how did they ever have time for any work? Maybe it's because nobody had invented television or computer games yet, so they had to do something to fill in the time between visits to taverns!

Anyway, as we go a little bit further up this steep hill, we come to Ivy House where Anna Pavlova, perhaps one of the world's most famous ballerinas lived from 1912 to 1931. This little house has had an interesting past, going from a ballerina's home to a part of Middlesex University (appropriately enough attached to the speech and drama department).

Hampstead Village

This is now the beginning of Hampstead Village itself. If we pass the Hare and Hounds on the left (because although very pleasant it is not particularly interesting) we come to the Old Bull and Bush which had its origins in 1645. It has to be said that it has changed a lot since its humble beginnings as a farmhouse selling ale (this explains the name – Bull for the farm, and Bush for the mandatory bush that was hung outside to say that a new batch of beer was ready.) At one time it is said to have been the country home of the artist William Hogarth (he is supposed to have planted the yew trees by the pub). Of course the pub has been the victim of many a "refurbishment" over the years, but at one time people such as Garrick, Reynolds, Addison, Gainsborough and Sterne would meet here for breakfast.

In the nineteenth century it was still frequented by writers, painters and actors and it is immortalised in the Florrie Forde song "Down at the Old Bull and Bush". Alas, gone are the days when sing-songs and concerts and sixpenny dances would be held in what were then the grounds. No more music hall at the Old Bull and Bush – you're more likely to encounter a karaoke evening now. But the little bandstand from which Florrie sang still exists in the car-park and it is still a splendid place to stop for a drink after a walk on Hampstead Heath.

A word of warning also to those people who object to looking at acres of healthy young people. A warm Friday and Saturday night at the Bull and Bush is only likely to remind you of whatever age you're the wrong side of. On the other hand if you're young, in Hampstead and looking for entertaining pubs to pop into, you could do worse than start here.

If you can now prise yourself out of the pub, turn left and continue walking by the heath. To avoid being run over, it is best to cross over the road here onto an elevated path on the right-hand side. Here you can't actually see the traffic, but unfortunately you can still hear it.

Not far from here is Wylde's Farmhouse, which I only mention because it is positively bristling with literary connections. Everyone from William Blake (who didn't like Hampstead even though he seemed to have spent a lot of time visiting the place) to Dickens to George Bernard Shaw seems to have popped in for visits of varying lengths. In the "how many famous authors have you had to stay?" competition which rages among buildings in Hampstead, the next house along is possibly a step ahead of Wylde's. At Heath House (corner of Spaniards and North End Road) the list includes George Crabbe, Wordsworth, Cowper with William Wilberforce the anti-slavery campaigner and Elizabeth Fry the prison reformer thrown in for good measure.

Jack Straw's Castle

The next pub is Jack Straw's Castle. The original building was badly damaged in the war, so was constructed in 1964 from some of the materials of the original pub with (as you would imagine) vociferous opinions from Hampstead residents. It has a rather grisly history though. The pub itself is named after Jack Straw, one of the leaders of the Peasants Revolt in the fourteenth century. The story goes that Jack Straw having set fire to the Priory of St John of Jerusalem in Clerkenwell, sensibly decided to get away from the scene of the crime as fast as possible. Hampstead seemed a quiet out of the way place as it probably was then – no pressure groups, no literary crush, just a few trees. Legend of course has it that as he settled down for a quiet old age, the King's Men came along and put a stop to him reaching any age at all. As if to reinforce this tradition of judicial execution the mantelpiece used to incorporate the gibbet which held the bones of Jackson, a notorious highwayman for many years. (Dick Turpin – who seems to have drunk in every pub in North London – is also said to have been a visitor but whether he did or not he may well have thought hard about drinking here since it was near to a popular execution spot for his fellow-highwaymen.)

Perhaps as a warning to modern politicians, John Sadleir, an MP in the mid-nineteenth, committed suicide behind the pub. Even in death, Hampstead has to revert to the picturesque – apparently all a suicide's goods and chattels revert to the lord of the manor. The unfortunate MP had nothing to call his own except the silver cream jug he swallowed the poison from. True to tradition the lord of the manor at the time exercised his right and claimed the cream jug (he did return it later.)

Nearly two hundred years ago, in the days before Hampstead became liberal and environmentally concerned the local hunt would also meet at the door of Jack Straw's before they charged off towards Hyde Park in search of foxes. If they could get through the traffic today they would do well – urban foxes are rumoured to be plentiful nowadays. Dickens also would (apparently) often ride out to Hampstead and once invited his biographer to join him for a "red-hot chop" and a "glass of good wine" (this explains the Dickens Restaurant in Jack Straw's). Thackeray, Stevenson and Wilkie Collins also frequented the place (you see, you get one writer round here and you just can't stop the rest coming along as well!) Gladstone also stayed round here for a short while, but since his house is now covered by the car park of Jack Straw's, there doesn't seem much point in dwelling on this further illustrious visitor.

Hampstead

Past Jack Straw's Castle going towards Hampstead you will come across a pond. Although these days on a Sunday it is mostly full of little (and big) boys playing with radio controlled boats, a clue to the pond's more practical purpose can be seen from the slopes leading into and out of the water from both directions. The pond was originally built for horses. The horse-pulled coaches would toil up Heath Street and then the animals would cool their legs in the water. If you have a mind (and a horse) to do so, try it for yourself . The horse of course will simply enjoy splashing through the water but this tends to upset the little boats (and the owners even more) but since all riders sincerely believe that horses have absolute right of way some heated exchanges could ensue. The army horses from the Barracks in St Johns Wood can often be seen walking through the pond in the morning on their way to exercise round the bridal path on the Heath extension. By the way in case you are thinking of bringing the car along to practice rally driving through the water there are now bollards to discourage motorists from taking a short cut.

Now we are coming to Hampstead itself (yes, finally). Walk on the right-hand side of the road past the two Metropolitan Water Board installations. Take a little diversion down Hampstead Grove for a bit of quiet past Fenton House which is one of the oldest buildings in Hampstead and now houses a collection of antique keyboard instruments. Turn into the Mount, which is an absolutely charming little road and you will pass the back of Coach and Horses. This pub, which is not one of the "famous" ones, boasts a lovely little garden so don't ignore it, just because it's not thronging with great ghosts. However, it must be admitted that the pub is much more attractive seen from the back!

Now we are passing Golden Yard which is part of the Ancient Manor of Hampstead and you can read for yourself the history of the Gouldings, the original owners. All the little roads around here are crowded with famous associations so it might be worth your while having a little wander before we get to the next pub. For instance, Holly Mount claims Dame Anna Neagle and George du Maurier as former residents while Holly Bush Hill can claim the internationally acclaimed Joanna Baillie. Yes, I know you're going to ask "Who?" Well, she was a playwright of the early nineteenth century whose fame has unfortunately outlived any interest in her work – luckily for her reputation, she is remembered for her friends, like Sir Walter Scott who walked all the way from London to see her.

Holly Bush Inn

All right, now we can go the pub. Walk up Holly Bush Steps to the Holly Bush pub and prepare to be delighted. This is a real old traditional inn, gas lit and reputedly on a site which had been home for a pub from 1630. The pub itself is probably too good to describe, but the story connected to it is well worth repeating (if only to give you something to read over your pint). The story goes that Romney, generally miserable and dissatisfied, despite having spent a considerable amount of time painting the delectable Emma Hamilton, decided to move to Hampstead to allow himself to be inspired to paint wonderful Shakespearian scenes. The whole episode was a disaster, ranging from the legendary slowness and expensiveness of builders to one of the artist's patrons making fun of him. The unfortunate Romney, who had come to Hampstead to escape from his depression, naturally very soon began to feel even worse and decided that his only course of action was to remove himself entirely from London and go back to die with his wife, whom he had left in the Lake District thirty-five years earlier. It is no wonder that his activities caused "great annoyance to his son"! The present Holly Bush Inn was converted from his picture gallery and riding-house and is still gas-lit. He had hoped to withdraw to the pure air of Hampstead, where he would experience an "hour of glory". Perhaps he can take some comfort in the pleasure that the pub now gives its lucky customers as many hours of glory as the licensing magistrates will allow. By the way, Dr Johnson used to drop by here as well when he was in the area and I don't think it's changed very much since he did!

If I have marched you through this part of Hampstead it is because there is so much to say about it. It is well worth more leisurely consideration. If you're too tired at the moment, go straight over and turn left down Hampstead High Street and you will be at Hampstead Station.

3. From Hampstead to Camden

Highlights: explore the deepest tube station in London, Hampstead High Street and Belsize Park; visit a Chinese Medical Centre and open-air markets.

Stations: Hampstead and Camden Town

Distance: 2¼ miles

By the time you have finished this walk, you will have come down in the world (geographically speaking of course) into one of the tackiest, noisiest and most vibrant districts you are ever likely to experience. Hampstead to Camden Town is a journey from outer to inner London – it is a reminder that the capital city, despite being full of ancient monuments is not a "heritage park" – it is still developing and districts change character even now. You can turn a corner and find yourself leaving the wealth of the upper middle classes to come face to face with real poverty. It is probably right to warn you that there is very little on this walk that is picturesque. Some of the pubs are a little "rough" but they all have a particular character which reflects what may be called a "cosmopolitan" population. This walk will probably act as a good antidote to the other side of Hampstead – where every house oozes money, charm and good taste.

The Walk

Starting off at Hampstead tube station (which happens to be the deepest tube station in London), as far as the purse can stretch there are pubs, restaurants and clothes shops styled to tempt the young and fashionable and those who wish they were. Come out of the tube

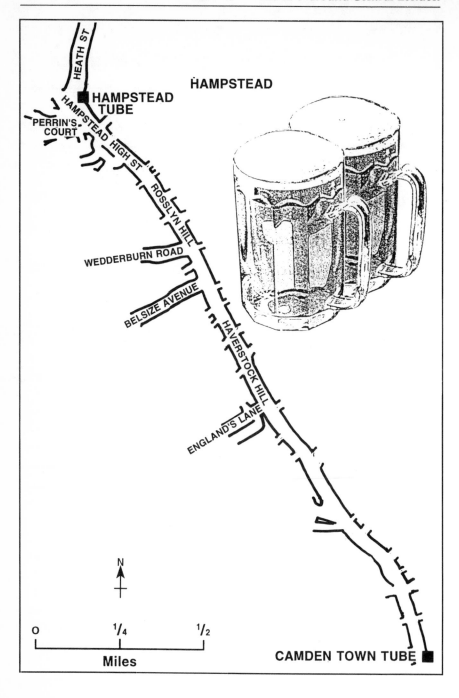

station and turn left down Hampstead High Street and look down the hill, past McDonalds, to The Dome, The William IV, and The King of Bohemia. The William IV (it is said) was named after the self-same King when he stopped on his way to Kenwood to eat strawberries in 1835. The King of Bohemia occupies a site which has boasted a pub since the seventeenth century – unfortunately the present structure dates back only a few decades. On the opposite side of the road take time to explore Perrin's Lane, Court and Walk, which was named after a local landowner and publican. As you would expect in a place which has been so fashionable for so long, there are plenty of places whose claim to fame is as the site of somewhere where somebody famous lived – so that as you pass the Greenhill block of flats on the right-hand side you may care to know that this is where Thomas Longman (of the publishing house) once lived and also died.

Rosslyn Hill

From the point where Hampstead High Street becomes Rosslyn Hill it's downhill all the way, in every sense of the word, as we go towards central London. Rosslyn Hill could easily be called a graveyard of interesting houses. There used to be on this piece of road interestingly named places such as the Chicken House (whose only real claim to fame was that James I and Duke of Buckingham stayed there one night in 1619 and it was very old). That disappeared in the last century – although not before it had been converted into an inn and became the "notorious haunt of thieves". Also on this stretch of road was Vane House once owned by Sir Henry Vane, who managed to upset both Cavaliers and Roundheads in the English Civil Wars and was beheaded by Charles II. One theory of the origin of the road's name even rests on a pub – the Red Lion – which disappeared in 1868 to be replaced by a police station and a drinking fountain. The other theory is that Rosslyn Hill is named after the Earl of Rosslyn, George Wedderburn, who lived near the road named after him and was so adept at changing his political allegiance that eventually the authorities had to give him an earldom and £4,000 per year to force him into retirement. But whether Whig or Tory, Wedderburn's certain claim to notoriety was his ferocity in sentencing political prisoners – it is said that he even "out-hung" the Hanging Judge Jeffreys himself.

So aside from remembering (with a shudder) such a pleasant character you may ask why "Why walk down here?" The answer is that for visitors (and even those who live in London) sometimes it is useful to see what can happen to a district even if it doesn't fall into complete decay. On Rosslyn Hill and as it becomes Belsize Park you can see the process as you walk – the traffic roar increases and the houses become bigger, gloomier and less chic. It's also true to say that if you are looking for eating places, Rosslyn Hill and Haverstock Hill cannot be ignored – everything from Israeli Falafel to French Cuisine is on offer at prices ranging from a joke to laughable.

As we go past the George on the left-hand corner by the Royal Free Hospital, refer to Walk number 7. Opposite the George is Wedderburn Road, only interesting because as we have already seen it is named after one of the most accomplished turncoats of all time.

Belsize Park and Haverstock Hall

We are now in the area called Belsize Park but on the right-hand side of the road you will see Belsize Avenue. Nowadays this area is made up of a cluster of Victorian villas, to a large extent let out in bedsits to a nomadic population of students and the like (these contemporary tenants may like to know that in the sixteenth century you could rent the whole area for £19. 2s. 10d and ten loads of hay). Centuries ago this area was occupied by Belsize House, home to various generations of various families who were slightly notable for holding such worthy jobs as Clerk of the Council to Elizabeth I and Gentleman of the Bedchamber to Charles II etc. One of these early owners did manage a rather exciting voyage to Newfoundland in 1536 where the ship's crew began to eat each other in extreme hunger. Later on those two famous diarists Pepys and Evelyn disagreed about the gardens (Pepys – "the most noble I ever saw"; Evelyn "very large, but ill kept"). True to Belsize Park form the place went downhill early in the Eighteenth century firstly in 1700 when a chapel was built in the grounds to enable couples to celebrate their weddings there for 5s. 0d (25p) provided they had their wedding breakfasts in the park and then, in 1720, when it was opened up to the public as a place of summer entertainment. Horse races, stag hunts, carp fishing, gambling tables – as you would expect every conceivable type of fun was provided (with the secure knowledge that "twelve stout fellows completely armed" [later increased to thirty] had been employed to "patrole" so no trouble would occur. The venue became so popular that even the Prince and Princess of Wales were to be seen there with the result that on at least one day three or four hundred coaches carrying nobility packed the grounds.

All good things must come to an end. It soon became notorious for "unlawful gaming, riots and dissipation". It was later put back into private hands (where it descended so far into respectability that a future prime minister actually lived there!) However, this is still Hampstead, which tries to be a little bit different, so we should note that this distinguished resident was in fact Spencer Perceval who was later assassinated in the House of Commons. The house was demolished in the middle of the last century.

Next, we pass Belsize Park tube station on Haverstock Hill. Look out for the Haverstock Arms and its extraordinary mural of a brewer's dray on the brickwork – the shire horse looks deformed (maybe it was forced to walk up the hill?) But the blank wall would be a very bleak prospect without it!

You will now pass England's Lane on the right-hand side. Down this road (which was once indeed a leafy country lane) there is the Washington, a pub which deserves a visit to look at the superb Victorian mirrors and the wood panelling inside. Arthur Rackham also lived here briefly before moving round the corner.

Next in the list of famous people who have lived in Hampstead (although I personally feel this is getting to the outer limits of the best end of it!) is Sir Richard Steele, the early eighteenth-century essayist who is now known as the founder of the magazine 'The Spectator'. He lived in a cottage here but in common to so many other things in this part of the world it was demolished to make way for a road. (Steele also used to spend a lot of time at the 'Kit-Kat Club' which met at the top of Heath Street.) The pub which bears this man of letters' name, is Steele's and is undoubtedly aimed at the younger set. It also includes one of the few pub breweries to be found in London (and even more unusual seems to be independent of any larger brewery). It is called West's Brewery Company Limited. I leave beer enthusiasts to judge the quality of their product (as they no doubt will!)

On the opposite side of the road is The Load of Hay, briefly known as The Noble Art to commemorate its earlier role as the home to the Belsize Boxing Club (and gymnasium). One of its more interesting landlords seems to have a gentleman so rotund that the only place large enough to "store" him when drunk was on the bar. He must have been no bother in his cups, because one evening it was only when they tried to wake him at closing time that they realised he was dead! Surely this must have been one of the most apt uses of the phrase "Dead drunk".

Haverstock Hill is really beginning to get tatty now, and we will soon be into what has become one of London's recent additions to the tourist scene.

You can find quirky shops like the Centre for Traditional Chinese Medicine and next there is Chalk Farm and the Roundhouse, a former engine shed which still sits in isolated splendour waiting for somebody to decide exactly what to do with it. Playwright Arnold Wesker gave its fortunes a brief revival in the sixties with his Centre 42, and I remember going to see some quite anarchic theatrical productions there (unfortunately none of which made enough lasting impression for me to remember what they were called).

I think it also used to house "happenings" – another flower-power phenomenon associated with crushed velvet flares and smelly Afghan coats. Perhaps it is only appropriate that many of these idiosyncratic fashions have been revived and now hang on stalls in Camden Lock a few yards up from the Round House (the original coats have probably now mercifully reached a final resting place).

Camden Town

If you are of a "certain age" Camden is the place to reincarnate your lost youth (unless you want it to stay lost, in which case stay out of the market and stick to the pubs!)

And there are plenty of them, including a new brew pub in the Firkin chain (alas no longer owned by the beery genius David Bruce but passed into the hands of Allied Breweries) as you walk down through Camden you can visit The Engine Room, The Monarch, The Man in the Moon (looking curiously traditional while most of the other pubs are trying to look anything but!) The only warning that needs to be given is that the place is heaving (outside the pubs, sometimes literally) on Saturdays and Sundays as native shoppers and tourists from other parts of London as well as from elsewhere pick and shove their way round the new two-storey market and the older open air jumble of entertaining tat. Don't expect to find a bargain – the stuff only looks cheap.

As you walk along, there is plenty of evidence of Camden Town's most recent less cosmopolitan past but very little, alas, of the days when it was a rural dream – running brooks, cattle grazing, trees, clean air. These days even a window box would have a tough time surviving the traffic fumes. The pawnbroker's sign on the corner of a side street speaks volumes of the area's descent from relative affluence as a haven for the comfortable professional classes 150 years ago to its current uneasy mix of poverty and trendy money. I expect there are still fights on Saturday nights outside the pub, but nothing to compare to the romantic duelling which used to take place around here. In fact it was known for it – back behind what is now Chalk Farm station, duelists used to order breakfast in the

Chalk Farm Tavern and then set to trying to kill each other under a nearby row of trees. The local constabulary found an easy way to increase their productivity ratings by hiding in a conveniently situated ditch and popping out and arresting them.

Socially the pubs reflect the schizophrenia of the area, ranging all the way from social classification ABC1 (the full gamut of the commercially interesting middle and upper classes) to E (no money, no job and no likelihood of getting one). It's well worth looking up behind the grotty exteriors to see the original brasswork above the windows of the Rock Tavern and the stonework which the Buck's Head hides underneath the jumper stall outside.

Eventually you will come to the World's End and the Halfway House just by Camden Town station.

4. Smithfield Circular

Highlights: the setting for 'Oliver Twist', the London House of Correction, Hatton Garden, Smithfield Market, a Lord Lucan connection . . . and plenty of sleaze!

Stations: Farringdon Road

Distance: 2 miles

This has to be the sleaziest walk of the book. At least it would have been if you had been doing it a few hundred years ago when this area catered for the most down-at-heel end of the leisure industry.

The Walk

As you come out of Farringdon Road Station, walk along Turnmill Street. Looks innocuous? Imagine it three hundred years ago, when twenty-one alleys opened into this quiet little backwater and seventeen different inns overflowed with whores, thieves and drunkards. The whores, poor girls, had to work extremely hard since they were paying something like 40 shillings (£2.00) per year for their miserable rooms – this was extortionate since even two hundred years later 6d was regarded as perfectly adequate payment for a whore's services. No wonder the poor girls were worn out after a few years and had to "seek harbour in a hospital". Don't, of course, let this put you off Turnmills on the corner. It is a perfectly respectable establishment!

Clerkenwell Green

Rather, carry on over Clerkenwell Road and into Clerkenwell Green. This Green of course hasn't seen any grass for about two hundred years and it is fairly quiet these days. Instead of the trees which once ringed what was once the Village Green, there are now parking meters but we are now in an area described in all its awfulness by Dickens – particularly in Oliver Twist. Mysterious sober-suited men carrying what look like foreshortened brief-cases abound at certain times. But they are only about to roll up their trouser legs, not because they're going to go paddling in what used to be a mill-stream under ground but because the large imposing building at right angles to Clerkenwell Road is a Freemason's centre. This building was once Clerkenwell Magistrates Court where Oliver Twist was tried for theft. The dungeons now house a bar and restaurant open to the public.

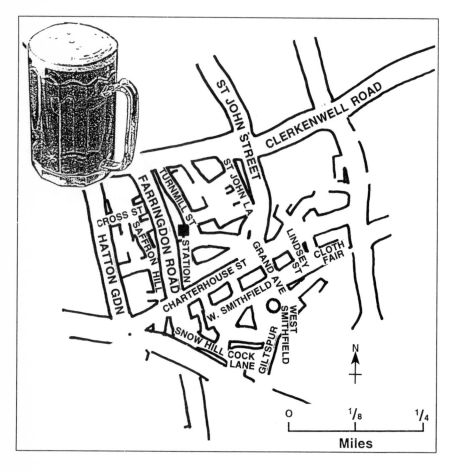

Or you may prefer to turn into The Crown Tavern, a well-restored Victorian pub. Alas, all that is on display in the pub now is the "Ryehouse Clock", which, legend has it, was the very clock used to tell when it was the correct time to assassinate Charles II and his brother, the Duke of York (later James II). The Ryehouse plot was an unsuccessful plot to kill the pair and replace them with the Duke of Monmouth to assure the Protestant succession. Historically worthy as this memento may be, a previous exhibit, a mummified cat, complete with desiccated rat within its jaws may have been more exciting. Although it may well have put you off your beer.

Rather more likely to encourage merriment was the Apollo Music Hall which took place upstairs in the pub. I have heard (and I have absolutely no proof) that there are underground tunnels in the Crown leading to the old Clerkenwell House of Detention. This has now been opened as a new tourist attraction in Clerkenwell Close as The London House of Correction (1616 – 1896). Among the more glamorous inmates of the prison was Jack Sheppard the highwayman (who, with his mistress, romantically sawed his way to freedom through the bars). Rather less inspiring were a pair of Fenians who were subject to a far less successful escape plan. Their associates attempted to blow up the prison, but managed instead to only demolish one of the walls, a row of houses, kill six people and injure fifty more. Despite this wholesale destruction, they unfortunately still did not set their friends at liberty!

Saffron Hill

After this excitement, it is time to go back to Clerkenwell Road, turn right, cross Farringdon Road and take the first left which is Saffron Hill,(another part of this area which has a history of vice and iniquity). It was round here that Dickens' Oliver Twist was introduced to his life of crime. Even earlier than this Saffron Hill was notorious for "lascivious and shameless women . . . who sit usually at their doors [to] shamefully allure such as pass by". As far as I can tell there are few attempts to allure anyone anywhere these days unless it be into Hatton Garden which is immediately at the end of Saffron Hill.

Hatton Garden

The allure of Hatton Garden these days is of course the sparkle of diamonds (and I suppose if we were romantic, the love-light in the engaged couples' eyes as they view the treasures through jewellers' windows). Originally the top half of the street (i.e. nearest Saffron Hill) was guaranteed shop free and contained such little gems as a Charity School (you can still see the little figures of the pupils in the preserved facade just by Cross Street). But there's not much left of what was a very pleasant and "esteemed situation for gentry". That is until you get to an almost unnoticeable lamp-post, adorned with a small mitre which leads you into a small alley.

Ely Place

Turn down here for what is a real highlight of this walk. For here we are in Ely Place and Ye Olde Mitre. The first thing to remember when you enter into this little part of history is that you are not in London, but in fact in Cambridge. Because the land here was originally owned by the Bishop of Ely and it became part of his jurisdiction. One of the main benefits of this was residents' exemption from taxation – but don't rush to sign up to live here. That particular liberty disappeared in the nineteenth century. It is still technically a private road, with a gate house and a commissionaire. Police are only permitted in by invitation. Which of course does not affect Ye Olde Mitre Inn because it is an establishment of the utmost respectability – there isn't enough room to swing a decent sized cat in the bar, let along have a brawl! On the other hand it might be a good place to hang about in if you think you're about to be served with a writ!

The pub which was built in 1770, replaces the original tavern built in 1546 which (so the rumour goes) originated in the buttery which was established in the crypt of St Ethelreda's Church. The resulting

noisy drinking parties put the Bishop off during Divine Service so he established the new pub out of earshot. There was evidently a lot of merriment associated with this little tavern – the cherry tree preserved in the corner is supposed to be that which marked the boundary between the Bishop of Ely's property and that of Sir Christopher Hatten. Sir Christopher who was one of Elizabeth I's favourites, got the place on very favourable terms – one red rose, 10 loads of hay and £10 per annum. Perhaps it was when he was having his house-warming party that Elizabeth was supposed to have danced around the tree with him – a nice thought! Whatever the truth of this, the man who built the table in the bar must have been drunk – it is, apparently, too big to go out through the door.

Unfortunately, other people did not find the place so amusing and these probably included the prisoners kept inside the pub during the Civil War, particularly since the bar was no doubt closed. Still in the Civil War the place served as a hospital as well. Poor William Cowper the poet, also came here to study law with a local solicitor in Ely Place, but found the place so depressing he had to leave London altogether. Perhaps he should have spent more time in the bar and less time with the lawyer!

Probably more relevant than any of this to the hungry walker is the fact that the pub's sandwiches have been given the Egon Ronay mark of approval – and they're still really good value!

But we can't stay here all day – there are exciting places to go. So make your way out of the bar out into Ely Place, turn left at the top, continue past the bottom of Saffron Hill, with Shoe Lane on your right, and you are now coming into Charterhouse Street, Smithfield Cellars and Smithfield Free House are on your right. Continue down Cowcross (aptly named as you will soon find out) and past the Hope Tavern with its ornate facade, just one of the many pubs round here which seem to have had extraordinary amounts of money lavished on them when being built as Victorian palaces devoted to brewers' profits.

Smithfield

There is so much to say about Smithfield it is difficult to know where to start – but maybe early in the morning at the Fox and Anchor is a good time, and it's a good place as well (but there is a lot of walking to do first so don't look for it quite yet). For it's one of the pubs around here where the curiously archaic English licensing laws have been bent to cater for those of you who like to have huge cooked breakfasts and drink Guinness at 6.30 in the morning. I hear the groan. You don't have to go there at 6.30 – it's just that's when you can see the meat market in full swing and that's when the pubs which hold a "market licence" open.

It is only fair to point out now that if you are of a squeamish nature or a committed vegetarian, avoid this part of the walk or at least make sure you start it after 2.00 pm – we are about to venture into one of the best known meat markets in the world.

At least you can feel thankful that now the animals are already butchered before they get here. Do we all remember from our school-days Dickens' description of Oliver Twist's journey through Smithfield in the tender hand of Bill Sykes? In those days (the 1830s) says Dickens "The ground was covered, nearly ankle-deep, with filth and mire; and a thick steam, perpetually rising from the reeking bodies of the cattle . . . "; no, I won't go on – it may put you off your next drink and there are so many interesting pubs around here that that would be a shame.

St Bartholomew's Hospital

There isn't time here for more than a very shortened history of Smithfield, but it grew over the centuries from a Saturday horse-fair and cattle market to what it is now. In 1123 it acquired St Bartholomew's Hospital founded by Rahere, a monk who had gone from minstrel-playboy to seriously-minded fellow when he caught malaria on a pilgrimage and promised that if he got better he would found a hospital for the poor of London. Fortunately he did get better, the hospital was founded and thrived with such people as Sir Richard Whittington, Lord Mayor of London and well-known cat-fancier, who left money for its upkeep in his will. During Henry VIII's reign it was valued at the extraordinarily large sum of 35 pounds 5 shillings and 7 pence. Henry, who seems to have had a lot more care for the health service than some more modern administrators, decided that the hospital could not possibly be closed along with the neighbouring monastery, and therefore refounded it with provision for 100 beds and a permanent medical staff. A rating system was introduced to fund the hospital and by the seventeenth century, enormous medical advances were being made. Imagine, not more than one patient was allowed to each bed and liquor could not be sold to patients without their doctors' consent! (Later, rules got even tougher – patients caught drinking alcohol in the hospital were summarily discharged – whatever their state of health!)

Rahere was also granted a licence to hold a fair for three days each year around St Bartholomew's Day to help provide some revenue to support the hospital. This fair later became one of the most notorious London celebrations, inspiring both wrath from the Authorities and a hysterically funny play from Ben Jonson.

While you're here have a look at Greenhill Rents and Albion Court.

Past the Bishop's Finger on your right, you will go down East Poultry Avenue and past the Cock Tavern. This once apparently opened at 4.00 am to provide thirsty market workers with their speciality, a "wazzer". This was a mixture of hot tea and whiskey, designed presumably to stun their taste buds into submission until the other taverns opened so comparatively late!

But in earlier days it did have a function on Friday afternoons, as the place where Victorian Costermongers would buy their donkeys and ponies. You could buy everything from the donkey to the cart here, at any price from 5 shillings to 3 pounds. The din was deafening. Mind you, however noisy it got, one thing was guaranteed to shut people up – when a stray bull from the meat market came trotting by, the costermongers would disappear to safety "for fear of being taught the hornpipe"!

Just near here Cock Lane is interesting to ponder on for two reasons. At the risk of sounding coarse, it must be pointed out that other streets in this part of the world were named after the professions carried on in them, so that it is easy to see how Cloth Fair and Hosier Street achieved their names. Shall I leave you, gentle walkers to draw your own conclusions about the origins of Cock Lane's name? I will simply point out that in 1241 the City authorities designated this charmingly appointed street as an "assigned place"; that is, somewhere to shove the City whores when they wanted to clean up the City streets. Of course, at Fair time, they obviously served a need, operating out of tents with queues of customers waiting for their go at the "Bartholomew Babies". But at least they weren't expensive – Samuel Pepys had his way with one in his coach for a shilling. Charles II is also supposed to have popped in for quick one – and had his pocket picked in the process (unlike modern royalty he apparently carried money on him) after which his unexpected lack of funds did not please his partner in the transaction!

There is the statue of a little fat boy perched above the corner over the sign declaring Cock Lane. This marks how far the Great Fire of London reached before it stopped.

It is probably about time we raised the tone of this walk again, so perhaps we had better move along to Cloth Fair past the Betjeman Wine and Eating House and also have a look at the Barley Mow (reputed to be one of the haunts of Lord Lucan) and then the extraordinarily well-restored Rising Sun in Rising Sun Passage. You must look at the trompe-l'oeuil windows on the first floor.

The Hand and Shears

At the corner of Middle Street and Kinghorn Street is situated the Hand and Shears which really does have an ancient and interesting history, inextricably tied up with both Bartholomew Fair and the tailors who frequented these parts.

It was firstly the place from which the Lord Mayor of London traditionally opened the Fair. Among other things drinking a pint of wine with the Keeper of Newgate Prison was the order of the day, (unfortunately one Lord Mayor did this so enthusiastically that the sound of a tankard closing frightened his horse, he was thrown and he died the next day!) Other more fortunate dignitaries lived to tell the tale and in fact the pub was also the site of the ancient Pie Poudre Court (a name derived not from baking ingredients but from the Norman French for "dusty feet") This was a temporary court held to issue drink licenses for the booths, deal summary justice to fair-goers and operate as a weights and measures office.

There were of course lighter moments for the pub during the Fair (depending on your definition of "lighter"!) It provided a focal point for processions and rallies, such as the tailors' own march which drove local residents mad by banging their shears and ringing their door bells on the night before the fair.

Another tradition was the Lady Holland Mob. This procession, which assembled at the Hand and Shears eventually attracted some 5000 people who carried an effigy of a Cavalier lady who had given shelter to Bartholomew Fair players from the Puritan zealots of the Commonwealth.

By the eighteenth century, opening the Fair had become a theatrical extravaganza complete with trumpets, drums, fiddles, harlequins and columbines, punch and the devil and play-emperors and kings.

True to form, the Victorians were horrified at so many people having such an uncontrolled good time and promptly banned the whole thing in 1855. I can't think of a better word for them than "spoil-sports".

At this point there is no use in regretting what the Victorians banned and simply look back at the view down Cloth Fair.

St Bartholomew's Church

Now go into Bartholomew Close and go round the back of Bartholomew Church. The Church is extremely interesting and should not be missed – if only because of its multitude of distinctly non-ecclesiastical uses, from coal and wine store to private house, printers workshop (where Benjamin Franklin once worked) and a blacksmith's forge. The ghost of the founder of the monastery and the hospital is said to walk (or rather hop) here apparently because he only has one sandal in his grave. Now walk through Middlesex Passage, turn left through a little gateway, then through another little gateway and we are now in Little Britain.

Originally named after the Dukes of Brittany (and therefore not remotely patriotic) this little lane used to be full of booksellers, including the one who failed to get anyone to buy Milton's Paradise

Lost and the one whose pretty wife Samuel Pepys liked to kiss. 'The Spectator' was born here, Dr Johnson came here with his mum when he was three, and Wesley was converted to evangelicalism here. Such excitement in such a small street!

Smithfield Executions

At the bottom of Little Britain, cross Smithfield (sparing a thought for its human victims – for four hundred years Smithfeld was a place of public execution with various recipes for criminal-of-the-day. They could be boiled in oil or water, roasted in a cage, or simply, if unimaginatively, hanged). Prisoner transport had not quite reached up to the currently high standard of police van. In days gone by one "deceiver . . . secret murderer, filthy fornicator, pollutor of concubines and false accuser of his elder brother" was dragged all the way from Cheapside by his heels to be hung at Smithfield. That one probably drew a good crowd! The crowds were enthusiastic and could reach as many as 20,000 for a particularly good spectacle, such as when Jack Ketch the notorious hangman was himself executed in 1686.

The Market

Turn right up Long Lane, past Ye Olde Red Cow and then into Lindsey Street. Walking past Smithfield itself you will see that it is being restored to a splendour it perhaps hasn't seen since it was opened in 1868. This temple to carnivores, originally modelled on the Crystal Palace is currently also being discussed at European Community level, whose hygiene regulations are threatening to close it down. Ignore the controversies if you can and take a look at Grand Avenue in the centre of the old market. When the traders have gone in the afternoon look up to the sky through the glass roof and consider this. 172,000 tons of earth were removed to build the railway underneath this building, the gates are each twenty-five feet high, nineteen feet wide and weigh fifteen tons. I think (and you don't have to agree) that maybe we can forgive the Victorians for ending the annual Bartholomew Fair since they put this in its place.

You will now find yourself in Charterhouse Street, and you will have a choice of two taverns (you don't need to choose of course – go into both!). The Smithfield Tavern advertises its allegiance to the market with its cows and goat heads displayed proudly over the door.

Fox and Anchor

The Fox and Anchor next door has an even more splendid front. Now preserved, the pub has been photographed (and exhibited) by Prince Richard of Gloucester, it used to hold cookery expert Clement Freud's wine cellar and it also claims (with no proof it has to be said) to be one of the stopping off places for the criminals on their way to be hanged at Smithfield. Let's hope they had time for one of the truly gargantuan breakfasts. It is unfortunate that you may have to fight your way through city workers stoking up before the rigours of the office, but bury yourself in the black pudding and the mountains of toast, the specially-made sausages and the eggs and a state of blissful sated oblivion will be achieved (indigestion will probably follow – but who cares?)

If you've had enough to eat now, we'll carry on. If you really feel in need of a rest sit for a while in the park at the end of the road.

Charterhouse

Previous occupants will not bother you, particularly the 30,000 or so plague victims who are buried underfoot. As part of a Carthusian Monastery, live inmates kept to a strict vow of silence. Sir Thomas More lived here for four years, trying out this strict way of life. Although a very religious man, he realised he could not go through life without some "pleasures of the flesh" and left to get married. He also invented Utopia (where it was recommended that all engaged couples should have a good look at each other naked before marriage) although I am sure he never indulged in such things, particularly with the unpalatable ladies of Turnmill Street! Clearly celibacy, silent and solitary confinement were not for him! However, as he finally lost his head on the matters of religious principles and the number of wives Henry VIII could be married to at any one time, perhaps he did learn a thing or two from the monks.

St John's Gateway

You probably need some company now so back past the Fox and Anchor and turn right up St John's Street. Cross carefully and go up St John's Lane where we will meet our old friend Dr Johnson yet again. You really can't go far in this part of London without bumping into his presence.

St John's Gateway which stands before you has a long and naturally chequered history. It has been everything from a monastic institution, home The Knights of the Hospital of St John of Jerusalem, to the Elizabethan Censor's office, where William Shakespeare and friends would have to trudge with their scripts under their arms to place their works under the scrutiny of the Master of the Revels. They were far more worried about religious and political impropriety than smuttiness – keeping sedition under control was far more important than a few off-colour jokes!

St John's Gate retained its intellectual associations over the next two centuries (with a period of dilapidation in the middle) becoming a coffee house run by the painter William Hogarth's father (who would happily quote Latin to his customers – can that have been good for trade?) and then the headquarters of a magazine written largely by – yes you guessed it, Dr Johnson. I trust, gentle walker, that you too, like Dr Johnson will behold this gate "with reverence". On his death bed Johnson referred to his boss on the Gentleman's Magazine, on which he worked at the Gate as a "penurious paymaster; he would contract for lines by the hundred, and expect the long hundred". Maybe if he had been paid better he would not have been kept writing behind a screen – apparently he was too scruffy to be on public view. But whatever his personal appearance (which was a little off-putting by all accounts) Johnson was one of the first journalists to report on parliamentary proceedings, albeit with as much imagination as accuracy.

The Gate became in turn, a pub and finally it has returned to its original use as a home for an Order of St John – although this time it is St John's Ambulance Brigade (who would probably have had their hands full if they had been on duty in the days of Bartholomew Fair!).

We can now stagger back along Charterhouse Street to Farringdon Road and the tube home.

5. Theatreland

Highlights: Leicester Square, Shaftesbury Avenue, Soho, Charing Cross . . . and the chance to meet a superstar or two!

Stations: Leicester Square and Temple

Distance: 2 miles

Now for a little glitter. Ladies, dab on the Chanel Number 5, slip into your best frock and practise balancing on the high heels. Gentlemen, prepare to escort your partners into the most exhilarating square footage in the world. We're going into London's theatreland and Soho.

And whenever you go into dangerous territory you should take a reliable guide, so I have provided Gerry Phillips, my next door neighbour, for you. He spent thirty years stage managing some of the biggest shows in London (Sound of Music, etc .) and has stored up a fund of stories about the great stars from the heyday of the West End musical, some of which can even be published! And since most of the stories seemed to involve going into the pubs, this seemed even more appropriate!

The Walk

Starting from Leicester Square station walk up Upper St Martin's Lane (believe it or not, until 1926 this was a well-known horse market) and into Monmouth Street (not the original Monmouth Street which now forms part of Shaftesbury Avenue and was famous as a centre for second-hand clothes) and stop at the Seven Dials. In the centre of the little opening is a replica of the original "Doric Pillar plac'd in the middle". The original one was removed to Weybridge in 1822. I advise caution in standing and staring at the pillar for too long as there seems to be some difference of opinion between those areas designated for cars and pedestrians in this particular little "square".

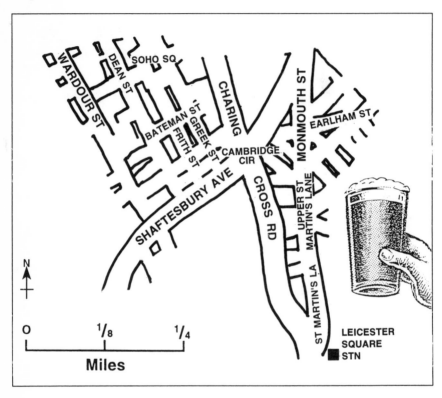

One place where you will be assured of a vehicle-free zone is the Crown pub on the corner. Here you can cheerfully ignore the traffic, enjoy the tiny bar and consider the type of person who might once have drunk here most of whom you would probably have preferred to see behind very different bars! Because despite the original intention that this area should be exclusively reserved for the fashionable and polite, by the nineteenth century it had become one of the centres for crime and prostitution in Dickens' London. Special escape holes were cut into walls so that a criminal could avoid capture simply by slipping out of the room without bothering to use a door. Over a hundred years earlier, John Gay author of the Beggar's Opera had written that round this area:

". . . the peasant with enquiring face
Bewildered trudges on from place to place
He dwells on every sign with stupid gaze. . . "

So let us leave our first pub, taking care to look intelligently at the street names and continue up Earlham Street where our second port of call (I think with the accent on the port – perhaps with a little touch of brandy) is the Marquis of Granby on the corner of Earlham Street and Shaftesbury Avenue. Before you go into the pub, you should probably have a look at the cockle and mussel stall, which is itself a venerable institution and has been for at least forty years. This is our first pub with theatrical overtones, since Ingrid Bergman used to go into the Marquis before her matinee at the Cambridge Theatre in "Month in the Country". As a true professional, she would only ever have one glass of wine. Just round the corner in Shaftesbury Avenue where Hoskyns House now stands, my friend Gerry remembers The Avenue Bar where he once took the Real Baroness Von Trapp (in National Costume) for a drink before she watched herself portrayed on the stage in the Sound of Music. Perhaps now she would have popped into the Limelight Club next door, where no doubt her dirndle skirts and bodice would not have excited attention or even a raised an eyebrow!

The Rudest Landlord?

Now we cross the road and we are entering into the realm of a landlord who has with great determination manufactured himself into a legend, as they say, in his own licensing hours, both lunchtime and evening sessions. Very few real pubs, I believe, have found their way onto the stage since the days of Shakespeare, but The Coach and Horses in Greek Street has featured on the London stage (in the play 'Jeffrey Bernard is Unwell'). But landlord Norman Balon, author of the literary classic 'You're Barred You Bastard!' and affectionately known variously as Nosey Norman and "The Rudest Landlord in London" has ruled the roost here for many years. His charming habits include swearing at customers, regularly sacking his barstaff (naturally expecting them to turn up for work the next day) and playing host to some of the great wits of the sixties, including the staff of Private Eye, who would invite distinguished guests to dine with them upstairs (including once Mrs Thatcher herself). Les Miserables is playing next door now, and I don't know whether the place is full of refugees from the French Revolution, but certainly when The Sound of Music was playing at the Palace, it was possible to meet the occasional nun in full costume at the bar.

The place has a rather dingy feel and is always packed. Although you are unlikely to brush elbows with celebrities such as Richard Ingrams, Jeffrey Bernard, Daniel Farson, and Danny la Rue, it is still worth a visit especially if you are hapless enough to enrage the landlord. The theory that the customer is always right has bypassed this corner of the West End – if you want tender loving care go somewhere else! – although the bar staff, as if by contrast, are exceptionally charming. Not a pub for the fainthearted, but certainly an original! In the heyday of the great West End shows the Greyhound next door used to get the overflow and was probably a comparative haven of peace and quiet. On Cambridge Circus itself, Londoners may remember that the Cambridge pub had the misfortune to fall victim to an IRA bomb a few years ago. Let's hope that is now a thing of the past.

Soho

It is quite difficult round here to find a pub which either does not have some fascinating anecdote associated with it, or failing this, has not had its fill of famous faces or is simply interesting in its own right.

For Soho has had a history which has encompassed every class of person and at some time has probably catered for every nuance of personal pleasure. To appreciate the full potential of the area, start by walking up Greek Street to Soho Square. The Square itself (created in the 1680s) was originally intended as a centrepiece for a very classy area and it remained so until the late eighteenth century when the really rich and famous left to make way for the professional classes. Charles II, who stands in the middle obviously found it all too depressingly middle class and was removed for a time to live with the Victorian W S Gilbert (who with his partner Arthur Sullivan created the well-known operettas), in Harrow Weald.

The Merry Monarch eventually found Middlesex far too boringly suburban and was returned to the centre of fun and frivolity in the late 1930s. Unfortunately, during his absence one of the houses, then round the square, witnessed the awesome spectacle of the

eccentric Joseph Merlin the inventor and the demonstration of the
first set of roller skates while playing the violin. I do not believe the
violin was an essential part of the equipment, merely an added
attraction. At any rate the demonstration came to an unfortunate
end when Merlin used a large and expensive mirror as a substitute
for his non-existent brakes. The damage was extensive and resulted
in an understandable lack of popular acceptance of his invention.
Charles II missed Merlin's radical personal transport system but
came back in time to see Soho gain its international reputation for
striptease shows and sleaze. The place has been considerably
cleaned up now but is still a great place to go for a night on the town
with a tremendous selection of restaurants, night clubs and other
fun and games.

To be honest, I am not sure this area should be "walked" in a rigid
way, because there are so many places that should be seen, perhaps
the best guidance to advise you to take your trusty map-book and
simply follow your instincts. But it is not right to leave you with no
help at all, so here are some ideas for places (and particularly pubs)
that you may care to visit. For instance, you can walk down from
Soho Square along Frith Street. This street has certainly had its fair
share of famous inhabitants, including Mozart, who would give
afternoon concerts here at the age of eight, William Hazlitt, the
eighteenth-century essayist, Charles Lamb (author of The Water
Babies) and another scientific demonstration of an invention that
changed the world. For it was in Frith Street that John Logie Baird
gave his first public showing of television.

To recover from the excitement of this scientific activity you will
probably need a rest, so now turn right down Bateman Street where
you will find the Dog and Duck, a pub which has been around since
1734. It's a very pleasant place but maybe its biggest claim to fame
is that it was here (can you contain your excitement?) that George
Orwell came to celebrate the fact that the American Book Club had
accepted Animal Farm as the Book of the Month. Wow!

But naturally, this is not the only pub in Soho that can boast
famous visitors. For instance the Admiral Duncan in Dean Streat is
where the artist Francis Bacon could once be seen in and then just

up the road is the more famous French House, now under new management, or the Golden Lion in Archer Street near the Windmill. This is where Quentin Crisp (before he became an international celebrity) would go. If you wish to delve a little further back in history, you might also want to look at The Crown and Two Chairman in Dean Street where (it is said) that Queen Anne's sedan chair carriers used to wait while she was having her portrait painted over the road at the studio of Sir James Thornhill. A likely enough story, but one does wonder (given the Queen's alleged fondness for alcohol) whether she went in to unwind after the stress of the sitting as well? Or perhaps they bought something over the counter for the journey home to the Palace. History, as so often is the case, does not recall.

Back to more recent times, the Duke of Wellington in Winnet Street has always been kept busy by its proximity to the stage doors of West End theatres – so you might meet at least a "budding" star there (if no reigning monarchs)! The White Horse in Rupert Street has also always proved very popular with theatricals particularly those working at the Lyric and the Apollo in Archer.

Dress sense

Parallel with Dean Street is Wardour Street, the heart of the British music and film business, and at lunchtime the streets are full of people from the industry. The Intrepid Fox does strike rather a radical note, and if you happen to wander past during the evening, you may care to try to get in "upstairs", although once you're up there you may wish you weren't (unless you have a penchant for "gothic" clothes.) Black lipsticks and fingernails and curious clothes made of bits of netting are de rigeur for the female customers (and very often the men). But don't worry that you will find yourself unawares in this strange and unearthly atmosphere. I have heard the story of one of the officials from the brewery which owns the pub not being allowed in because his suit and tie did not conform to their eccentric dress code!

It would not do not to visit the heart of theatreland, St Martin's

Lane, while in this part of the world so going south down Wardour Street turn left at the bottom into Shaftesbury Avenue. You are now at Cambridge Circus, so turn right down Charing Cross Road, and at Leicester Square find St Martin's Lane.

Here you will find the Salisbury a superb place which looks just as it should. It has seen everyone from Tony Armstrong Jones (who married Princess Margaret) to the actress Maggie Smith and a few more besides. The mirrors and brass work really should be seen, not described. It's all art nouveau, glittering lamps and plush seating. For those interested in its history, it was once famous for its prize-fights (at one time even being named after Ben Caunt – the man who is also immortalised in Big Ben).

For another pub touched with history you will have to find the stage door of the Coliseum where The Lemon Tree nowadays welcomes local office workers and theatre people. But it was apparently, one of the taverns Boswell first entered when he arrived in London from Scotland, being delighted to find that there was a landlord here from his home country. This is a story which I only found in one book, and therefore may be a little dubious in its authenticity – but it is a pleasant tale, so you must judge how accurate it is yourself!

From here you can take the tube from The Strand (or go back to the Salisbury to take in the glitter). This has been a short walk, but a fascinating one!

6. Hammersmith to Kew

Highlights: the places where "Rule Britannia" was written, telegraphy was invented, and where the mistress of Charles II is buried. See the Thames, walk down Chiswick Mall and admire some of London's finest architecture.

Stations: Hammersmith Broadway and Kew Gardens

Distance: 4$\frac{1}{4}$ miles

Both the Sun and the George pubs are on King Street. But before we talk about King Street itself, I must tell you the sad story of the Hammersmith Ghost who was sighted in 1804 and caused a sensation. The poor creature turned out to be a bricklayer with a new white jacket who frequently took a short cut through the local churchyard. The unfortunate man was subsequently shot dead by a local "ghost buster" (who was acquitted of murder).

The Walk

Walking up King Street, you will pass the Swan, which is a fine old pub. Continue walking until you go past the Hop Poles, which has amazing windows.

On the right is the Salutation which (it claims) was built in 1910 although there has been a Coaching Inn there since around 1750. Note the unusual blue tiles outside.

On the left, you will come to Nigel Place; take this road and then walk under the subway. Then out of the tunnel and turn left.

The Dove

Go into Furnival Gardens and then turn right down the little lane. Here you will find The Dove. The building itself dates from the seventeenth century and it was here that James Thomson the poet wrote the words for "Rule Britannia". Despite the song's celebraton of ruling the waves, water did not prove very lucky for him. He eventually died at the early age of 48 due to a chill caught on a boat trip from London to Richmond. This is another one of the pubs where rumour has it that Nell Gwynne and Charles II used to stop for a drink. Interestingly enough his widow and discarded mistress also lived just up the road as we shall see later.

The name, The Dove, dates from 1796 when it was opened as a coffee house. It is a charming low-beamed little place, exactly as you would wish a pub overlooking the Thames to be. It and the building next door were at one time one house, but it was split, with one half being made into a "smoking box" for the Duke of Sussex, who was Queen Victoria's uncle. I assume a smoking box is a gentleman's retreat – which would have been handy for Charles II!

The Upper Mall, Chiswick

Once you come out of The Dove, you will now find yourself on Upper Mall which at one time was the haunt of aristocrats and those who wished to mix in their society. Among the sometime residents of this fine riverside frontage were Catharine of Braganza (widow of Charles II) and one of his discarded mistresses, Lady Cleveland. History does not record (as it wouldn't) whether they ever met but I can't resist the thought of them out walking the King Charles Spaniels, and bumping into each other.

There were other less illustrious but more eccentric people around as well in those days, such as the man who invented the speaking trumpet and who subsequently got religious and buried £200 worth of music books below ground, which seems a rather curious way to prove your faith, but there you are.

We are now walking past Kelmscott House which witnessed the premature birth of the electric telegraph, invented by a man called Sir Francis Ronalds. When Sir Francis offered his breakthrough to the Admiralty in 1816 they politely turned him down saying that since they had just won the Napoleonic Wars they didn't really need a new telegraph system and they would stick to their flag based semaphore system, thank you very much.

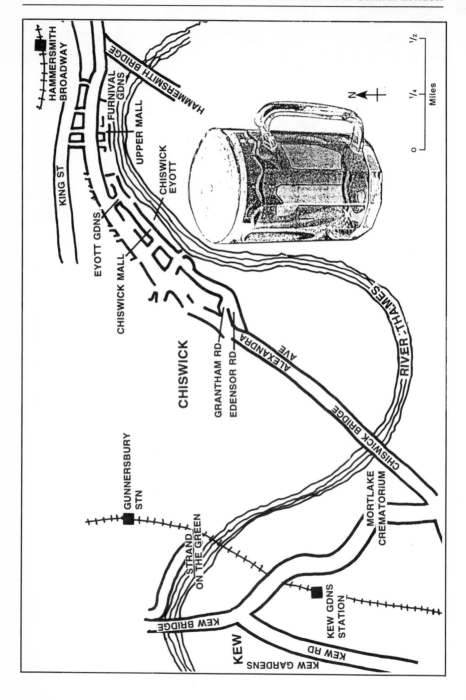

Ninety years later the house saw the death of the great designer, writer, poet, and campaigner William Morris. This was the man whose inspiration has covered millions of modern walls in paper "tapestries" of mediaeval flowers and created this house where, according to George Bernard Shaw, everything was "beautiful and beautifully presented".

Next to Kelmscott House is a Boathouse, which is appropriate because on this walk one of the great pleasures is watching energetic people rowing on the river. At this point look behind you to the Victorian Hammersmith Bridge which was saved from destruction just before the war by a quick-thinking passerby tossing an IRA bomb into the river. The river Thames now goes round the bend and we are in Upper Mall, Chiswick.

As you go along you pass Old Mill Lane and it is probably worth while pondering that on this lovely stretch of the river, at least the worst of the opposite bank is masked by trees. You will now be walking past The Old Ship which looks out over the river. With its splendid garden (also overlooking the river) it is well worth a stop. The walk beside the river stops for a while now and we have to turn right at the end but we come out onto a very pleasant turning which is worth some inspection (particularly the pub called the Black Lion which dates from the eighteenth century and still retains a skittle alley.)

Hammersmith Terrace

Then you must go down Hammersmith Terrace, if only to ponder on some of the people who have lived here such as the man who singlehandedly made modern NHS waiting lists pale into insignificance. He was Philip James Loutherbourg, originally a painter who turned to medicine in the late 1780s. His cures seems to have been a mixture of barley water and mesmerism, but he was certainly popular. Can you imagine 3,000 members of polite eighteenth-century society hanging around here picking up tickets and waiting their turn to see the great man? Unfortunately some time later the crowd turned ugly (presumably when they ran out of barley water) and chased the poor "doctor" out of the back door. As you can see by the blue plaques, there have been many more respectable inhabitants such as A P Herbert – but one has to ask oneself the question: "Have they been as much fun?"

Now walk down Eyott Gardens and then down Chiswick Mall. On the left through the gardens you can see the river again but to the right the houses are quite exquisite. On the left-hand side is the Chiswick Eyott which is an osier (or reed) bed. If you can smell beer from here it's because of the proximity of Fuller, Smith and Turner's Brewery. You are 100 yards from their back door.

Chiswick Parish Church

At this point you could actually get down onto the river bank if you want to, although at most times of the year, I would think it is a bit muddy. The next interesting place you will come to is Chiswick Parish Church, where stacks of famous people have been buried. William Hogarth lies here, along with many other people of whom you may never of heard. At least one other person worth seeking out is Charles II's mistress, Barbara Villiers, the Duchess of Cleveland. The unfortunate Loutherbourg, is also buried here – although he is no longer besieged by devoted admirers!

Out through the churchyard, take the footpath to Edensor Road. Unfortunately, this is not a particularly pretty part of the world, but bear with us and continue on to Grantham Road (it eventually gets better) and then right into Edensor Road, past the Chiswick Pool. Now go down to the traffic lights and left into Riverside Promenade. Turn left at the lights and this is Alexandra Avenue.

If you turn right at the next set of traffic lights this will take you to Chiswick House, which is well worth a visit. It is also not far from Hogarth's House, now a museum to the great artist.

Chiswick Bridge

We are now going to walk over Chiswick bridge, about which you can say very little except that it is just over sixty years old. At least as you walk along here you can look into people's gardens and see what they have done which may keep you interested.

Over the bridge there is the Stag Brewery with an extremely pleasant pub next to it which is called the Ship. This pub, which is Georgian, stands on the site of an Elizabethan tavern, and has had a variety of names, including the Hart's Horn and the Blue Anchor. However, (at least at the time of writing), it is now definitely called The Ship!

As we come into the Royal Borough of Richmond upon Thames you will find yourself walking past a selection of very fine houses, which would be well worth exploring. But now we are walking back under the bridge (where it can be a bit squelchy underfoot if it's been raining so it's probably best to bring your rubber boots). On the left-hand side there is the Mortlake Crematorium, as you will have noted by now there are a lot of cemeteries around here!

Just stand still and listen at this point – you can hear a strange mixture of quacking ducks, shouting, rowing coaches and traffic, with a descant of seagulls.

As you walk along you will pass the swimming baths and the Records office (neither of which are particularly riveting buildings) and you are about to go under a railway bridge.

Kew Bridge

If you cast your eye over to the other side of the river you will see Strand on the Green where there are a selection of super pubs including one which you will be able to see clearly called The Bulls Head. Unfortunately, you can't get to it but if you are really desperate to visit it just walk over Kew Bridge and then go straight back onto the opposite bank of the river.

You may notice that there are ropes hanging underneath the bridges. These are to help boats negotiating the river at high tide so that they know how much clearance there is.

The buildings improve considerably round about here with a pretty row of houses on the left-hand side. We are now just coming up to Kew Bridge. Kew Gardens are straight ahead but we will be turning left here and if you need to, you can stop for a drink. There are a variety of pubs. On the right is Kew Green.

We will now be crossing the road to go round the back of the church. Cross back over again and walk down Kew Road. Despite the fact that this is a book which recommends you to stop at pubs for your refreshment, it would be wrong to leave out the little cake and tea shop you will now pass on the left. Here is Newins 'The Original Maids of Honour' bakery where you should buy yourself a cake. In this shop were made the original "maids of honour" which were served to Henry VIII and his household. Kew Gardens are on your right but we will turn left to Kew Gardens station.

Note that the standard of front gardens round here is particularly high!

Finally, just before you go home you may want to stop at the Flower and Firkin "free house" (which is in fact owned by one of the large national breweries). It has been charmingly done up and well worth missing a train or two for a chance to rest your feet!

7. Archway Road to Highgate

Highlights: Highgate Hill and Lauderdale House, one-time residence of Nell Gwynne. Highgate, famed for Betjeman, Faraday and Coleridge and Karl Marx. Visit a pub where Dick Turpin hid, enjoy the Vale of Health and see the olde English game of Pell Mell being played.

Stations: Archway, Hampstead Heath (BR) or Belsize Park

Distance: $3\frac{1}{4} - 3\frac{1}{2}$ miles

If I were being absolutely honest, I would have to tell you that the best way to start this walk is by bus. All you would really be missing is the Whittington Stone which is a small stone statue to Dick Whittington's Cat. Whittington (with what must have been excellent hearing!) is said to have heard Bow Bells (situated some miles away) chime "Turn again Whittington, thrice Lord Mayor of London" and is then supposed to have made his way down Highgate Hill on his path to riches (and everlasting fame as a pantomime hero) accompanied by his feline friend. In truth, you are better off seeing this stone from the top of a bus anyway since the inscription giving Whittington's dates as Lord Mayor is misleading. Firstly, the legend of Whittington's coming to London as a poor country boy seems to have no basis in truth; secondly he was Lord Mayor four times; and, last of all, did you ever hear of a cat leaving home and all those tasty country mice to walk to London, however attractive its owner looked in tights and thigh-length boots?

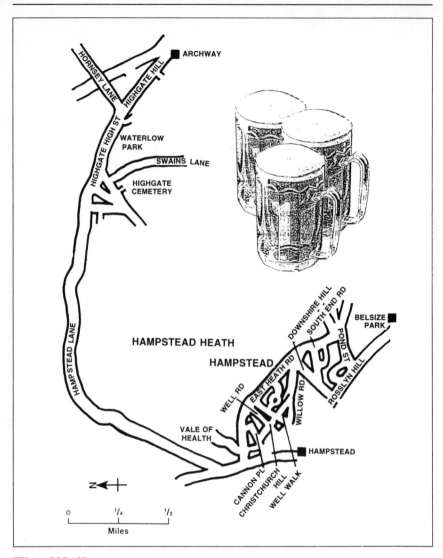

The Walk

As this really isn't the most scenic area in London, when you get out of Archway station, you're allowed to take a bus up Highgate Hill, provided you get off before the road becomes Highgate High Street. Otherwise you will miss some good stories and, probably more importantly, some very good pubs! On the right-hand side on the corner of Highgate Hill and Hornsey Lane is the Old Crown. Just past this junction is Waterlow Park and Lauderdale House (where you can get a good cup of tea and a sit down before you tackle the Highgate pubs!)

Lauderdale House

The legend goes that Charles II borrowed Lauderdale House for Nell Gwynne who, anxious to obtain some sort of recognition for her child by the King, held him out of the window and threatened to let go unless the Merry Monarch gave him a title. "Save the Earl of Burford" was the legendary reply. The lad later became the Duke of St Albans so obviously the experience had no detrimental effect on him (and it gave the gossips of Highgate something to talk about). Also round about here at the same period is said to have been sited the cottage of Andrew Marvell, the poet who gave us the immortal lines

"If we had world enough and time,
This coyness lady would be no crime"

Clearly, Mistress Gwynne, who referred to herself as "the Protestant whore" had taken his advice to heart!

Highgate Village

We are now coming into Highgate Village proper. This is Highgate High Street and this delightful road retains the charm of a (very expensive and exclusive) village street. Chocolate shops, dress shops, book shops, restaurants, everything is in the best possible taste! The pubs, however, are havens of a more plebeian culture and the Dukes Head on the right-hand side of the road and the Angel on the left will provide good value alternatives to the smart coffee shops and eateries.

As you walk down the High Street, you should take note of the coat of arms on number 42, next to Townsend yard and a courtyard with a very nice house down at the bottom.

Highgate, like Hampstead, has always been a haven of the finest minds and the likes of John Betjeman, the late Poet Laureate, Michael Faraday the distinguished Victorian scientist and Samuel Taylor Coleridge, author of "The Ancient Mariner" have all lived in Highgate. Even more of these brilliant (if dead) minds, found their way into Highgate Cemetery which you will find in Swain's Lane, a little way down this road and on the left.

Highgate Cemetery

Swain's Lane should carry a government health warning. Deceptively easy to walk (nay, roll) down, unless you are very fit it's desperately hard work walking back up it again. If you decide to make this diversion, you will be delighted by the monuments to such people as Karl Marx (the original motivator of so many now defunct governments). Does he receive so many visitors since Communism went out of fashion? A question worth asking – perhaps the Friends of Highgate Cemetery will know the answer! George Eliot is also there. Is she more popular since the BBC's film of Middlemarch? Another question worth asking, leaving us with the intriguing thought – what sort of fame lasts longer? Having a political movement named after you or being the inspiration for a TV series? Keep this thought until you climb back up to our route. You will need something to take you mind off the hill.

Also buried in the two halves of the cemetery (it proved such a fashionable place to spend eternity that they had to open an extension) are Tennyson's brother, Dickens' wife etc.

The western side is older and is closed except for official tours. It contains the most extravagant symbols of the Victorian way of death, overflowing with weeping angels and monuments to mourning.

Having struggled back up Swains Lane, turn left at the top of Swains Lane and you can see opposite over the other side of the square the back of the Prince of Wales pub. Go there if you wish but, however desperate you are after the climb, it would be as well to save yourself for the pub which is directly on your route. As you would expect here (if you have the strength to appreciate them) are fine houses and interesting houses everywhere but coming up on your right – past Bacon's lane which looks interesting – is a small terrace of houses which marks the back end of The Flask.

The Flask

The Flask is a delightful pub. Reputed to be one of the many pubs in which Dick Turpin hid (how did he ever get any highway robbery done?) it was refurbished a few years ago with the full cooperation of the local preservation society and provides a welcome haven after your exertions. It is said that the first inn on the site was built around 600 years ago. In those days it was sited on the main road into London from the North. The present building dates from 1767 but incorporates parts of a previous structure 100 years older. The pub naturally claims the usual list of famous drinkers including the same Karl Marx for whom the Flask eternally remains his local. Like its similarly named Hampstead rival, the Flask was one of the places where you could you get your bottle filled with health-giving Hampstead Well Water.

Swearing on the Horns

We also have to mention here the ancient custom of "swearing on the horns" which seems to be one of the most venerable examples of the "tourist trap" along with Spanish fiestas in the Costa del Sol and "Zorba the Greek" evenings on Corfu. The coaches stopped in Highgate. As they came in to London passengers would enter the various inns (of which the Flask was of course one) and the "Freedom of Highgate" would be mentioned. The naive newcomer was soon taking part in his initiation ceremony which involved basically, spending money in the pub, and taking an oath on a set of horns (ram, stag or bullock) to: not eating brown bread while you can get white, except where you like brown the best; not drinking small beer when you can get strong; not kissing the maid when you can kiss the mistress (preferably kissing them both!). The landlord would then command him to kiss the horns or a pretty girl if there happened to be one present.

At one time, this ceremony provided an entertaining day trip out for Londoners who would make up dinner parties in Highgate to initiate strangers, with as many as 100 to 120 being sworn in one day. The origins of the legend may have something to do with the toll customarily taken on sheep and cattle being driven to the London market transferring itself for amusement (and innkeepers' profit!) onto the passenger trade. There are still regular swearing ceremonies in the Highgate pubs, at charity evenings and the like.

Finish your drink and leave the Flask, turning right and then crossing over the road into the Grove. This attractive row of houses housed Samuel Taylor Coleridge (author of The Ancient Mariner) when he came to stay with his friend in 1816 and eventually died there 18 years later (one hopes he didn't just come for the weekend!)

Walk further on and at the top turn left into Hampstead Lane. If you turned right you would come to the Gatehouse, another pub famous for the swearing on the horns etc. recently re-opened after many years of neglect. It may be a good idea to stop here because there are not many pubs between here and our next stop! If you are going to stop here, it would be just as well to ensure you have either a child or an animal close at hand to ward off a possible sighting of the resident ghost, the murdered widow Mother Marnes. They say that actors do not like to compete with children and animals ... but ghosts is a new one!

We are now going down Hampstead Lane and you will be relieved to know that it's mostly downhill from here (in a literal sense of course – we're going to pass some pretty impressive property!)

Hampstead Lane

On the left-hand side on Hampstead Lane is Beechwood House a building dating from the 1820s. On the right-hand side you can see the back of the playing fields of Highgate School. The school was originally founded in 1576 and now is a well-known public school. (The traffic noise along here is absolutely dreadful – matched only by the noise of the boys when it's break time!)

On the left-hand side is Athlone house which is now part of

Middlesex Hospital, but has been in its time a military hospital, a nurses training school, and an Air Ministry building as well as a private residence.

Hampstead Heath

Carry on down the hill, past huge and impressive mansions and as you walk along look to the left over the heath. Traditionally one of the "lungs of London" this was one of the resorts where citizens could get the smell of the smoke out their hair and enjoy a good day out. The attractive undulating character of the heath is not as natural as you would think – to a great extent they have been caused by people digging out sand for brick making up to the middle of the last century. It was allowed to naturalise over leaving us with the present piece of land, beloved of North Londoners, with its bathing ponds, fairs and own particular brand of health-giving charm.

Kenwood House

We are now coming up to Kenwood House – on the left is the entrance. Despite the fact that this is not a pub, I think you should at least have a look at the outside. Since entry is free – you could even go in! It's well worth the detour to see this neo-classical house remodelled by Robert Adam and containing a breathtakingly magnificent library. There are many beautiful paintings on display in the house, including works by Rembrandt, Turner, Van Dyck and Gainsborough. There is also a lovely painting of an eccentric Englishman named Merlin, (see Walk 5), who seems to have invented the roller skate. At any rate don't be shy to ask one of the curators – they are remarkably friendly, helpful and, of course, knowledgeable.

But architecture is not all that Kenwood has to offer – there's an excellent tearoom in the Coach House and on Saturday nights in the summer there are open air concerts in the grounds which are crowded but fun. Picnic baskets sprout all round the grassy "auditorium", colourful tablecloths are spread out, champagne (well, fizzy wine) corks popping everywhere and all to a background of popular classical music and often spectacular fireworks displays. At other times there may be poetry readings in the house itself – it is well worth taking a look at what may be going on at the time you are planning to take this walk.

Assuming that you have not encountered such a cultural feast, after your tea leave Kenwood and turn left – continue down Hampstead Lane passing Bishops Avenue on the right. This road, known locally and elsewhere as "Millionaires' Row" (and sometimes "Burglars' Avenue") is full of huge houses inhabited by rich people from all over the world, some of whom use these houses perhaps for a couple of weeks a year if they happen to be in London (like a very expensive time share!). Perhaps this is the reason why at one time in the road there were hundreds of workmen around fitting burglar alarms!

The Spaniards Inn

After passing yet more expensive houses you will come to another famous old pub – The Spaniards Inn. Set just before the toll-gate which marked the boundary of the Bishop of London's lands, the building is around 500 years old. Naturally Dick Turpin is supposed to have stabled his horse in the toll house over the road.

The name itself is surrounded by mystery – perhaps it is named after the original Spanish landlords (two brothers), who are reputed to have fought a fatal duel over a young lady. Less romantically it may have been named after the Spanish Ambassador who occupied this building before it became a pub. On the other hand another story says that it was originally the old toll house! Again the literary associations become positively overwhelming – Goldsmith, Byron, Keats, Shelley, Lamb, Leigh Hunt and the artist Reynolds all popped in here for a drink. Dickens set the arrest of Mrs Bendell in Pickwick Papers in the garden. The ghosts of Dick Turpin and Black Bess (it is said) can be sighted on the road to the pub as they hurry towards their favourite hostelry but the pub itself, considering its age and exciting range of customers, is surprisingly phantom free.

One of the best (true) stories about the Spaniards Inn is "how the landlord averted a disaster". During the Gordon Riots of 1780 a mob came up to Hampstead to finish off Lord Mansfield who had escaped to his home in Kenwood House. On their way to the massacre, the rioters (who seem to have betrayed remarkably little staying power as rioters go) were invited in for a drink by the landlord of the Spaniards who plied them with beer and sent for the troops. By the time the army arrived, the rioters were not, it appears, in any fit state to offer much resistance! Guns used in the incident still hang on the wall of the pub (or maybe they belonged to Highwaymen – both legends are on offer!)

Carry on up the road which goes through the middle of heathland past Erskine house and Evergreen Hill which is where Cannon Barnett and his wife Dame Henrietta Barnett lived. Dame Henrietta was the guiding spirit behind nearby Hampstead Garden Suburb, the inspired experiment in residential town planning dating from between the wars which is a charming (but expensive) area of cottages and narrow streets.

The Vale of Heath

As you walk along you could take a footpath down to the left where you might see some of the army horses from St Johns Wood Barracks exercising on the heath – you will almost certainly come across joggers taking the name of this part of the Heath, The Vale of Health, very seriously. The Vale of Health is said to take its name from the supposed immunity of its residents from the recurrent waves of plague and cholera of earlier days, but since it was an undrained malarial marsh until 1777, the more likely reason for its name change is a need for a change of image! However, health hazards are more likely to come from the joggers so watch out – you are expected to get out of the way for them!

Continue on past the cycle way with a 8 mph speed limit (how do they enforce it?) past Jack Straw's Castle on the right-hand side of the road and the White Stone Pond. We will be turning left at East Heath Road. We are now standing higher than the cross on the top of St Paul's Cathedral and this was one of the sites of the early telegraph system of beacons which helped warn Londoners of the approach of the Spanish Armada to the English coast many hundreds of miles away in Plymouth. It is also the site of the Old Court House where local miscreants would be heard by the magistrates.

You will be pleased to know that the walk will be going downhill again for some time!

Hampstead

Continue down East Heath Road (single file here because Hampstead traffic waits for no man, woman or beast) and we are coming up to the Heath again and the Vale of Health. Just in case you have not had enough of distinguished residents yet, D.H. Lawrence came down here at one time, and the poet Percy Bysshe Shelley used to visit a friend here and sail paper boats on the local ponds. Since the unfortunate poet later died in a boating accident in Italy I think this was a rather ominous game to play.

Cross the road (very carefully) and you will see on the right, Squires Mount. At the top of Squires Mount is Cannon Place where Gerald du Maurier, the actor and father of Daphne du Maurier the author, lived.

If you then turn right at the bottom you will now be passing the parish Lock Up. This was of course a very convenient arrangement for the magistrate, who lived in Cannon Hall and held court there (the Lock Up was built into the garden wall) – he certainly would have been more comfortable than the prisoners who were kept in here until they could be dealt with more permanently. There are very few of these Lock Ups left in London – so look at this one carefully and just think how awful it would be after an over-indulgent evening in The Spaniards Inn to wake up in this dark, single cell with tiny barred windows and a thumping headache!

Now continue down Cannon Lane and at the bottom turn right into Well Road and you will find The White Bear, whose foundations date from 1704 and it therefore stakes a claim to be the oldest pub in Hampstead; however, it is only the foundations which are that old. It's quite an attractive pub, even though after refurbishment it smacks a bit of "pastiche history". Now turn left into New End Square and carry on down Christchurch Hill.

On your left is Burgh House which houses the Hampstead Museum, again worth a visit. It is named after a former owner, a London vicar who was so unpopular that his parishioners unsuccessfully petitioned Queen Victoria to have him sacked.

The Wells Hotel

On the left is the Wells Hotel (you will have to turn left into Well

Walk to get there) which is a reminder of the days when Hampstead provided fashionable London with its very own Spa. For Hampstead in the past was a place to "take the waters". These days the only remaining outlet for Hampstead water situated in Well Walk carries a warning that a passer-by should on no account drink from it! In fact the water proved so popular that flasks of the stuff were sent into London every day in the early eighteenth century. They could be purchased for a mere threepence per flask at a variety of local coffee houses, or for an extra penny they would be delivered to your door (naturally, like milk bottles the pubs expected their flasks back!). The Wells Hotel stands on the site of a pub named the Green Man, a little way from the site of the Wells Tavern – which at one time acquired a somewhat dubious reputation for being a place for irregular marriages but was also obviously a highlight of the Hampstead social life with its tea-gardens, dancing room, raffle-shops and bowling green.

After having a rest in the Wells Hotel, turn right down Christ Church Hill. Walk past the green, turn left and then continue down Willow Road. Although I can offer you no historical associations here, this can be a good opportunity to look (discreetly) into people's basements.

We are about to come out into South End Road and we are passing The Freemasons Arms on the right. This pub contains the last Pell Mell court in the country (Pall Mall takes its name from the game) so it's worth a visit for that reason alone!) It is a game requiring great concentration, so it is probably better to stick to orange juice if you want to play; on the other hand watching it does not require anything like such a clear head! It is a bit like croquet, but anyway see for yourself! The pub also has a skittle alley, another ancient game, which most people will recognise as the unmechanised version of tenpin bowling.

We are now in Downshire Hill which was developed in the early nineteenth century and as you can see still retains pretty cottage-style homes (unfortunately not available at pretty cottage-style prices!)

Walk enviously past Gloucester House on the right and now turn sharp left round past the church – this is St John, built at the same time as the road. It is unique in the Church of England in London because the lease of this chapel is owned by the congregation. Ten years after it was built in 1823 the Vicar of Hampstead took violent exception to the evangelical preachings of the incumbent clergyman and had it closed down despite a petition from local residents. It was closed for two years until the Vicar (who quarrelled "with the world") could find someone whose sermons were more to his taste!

Keats Grove

We are now in Keats Grove which of course is where the poet John Keats lived in Wentworth Place (1818-1820), at a rent of £5.00 per month and also met his fiancee Fanny Brawne. If you are of a sensitive nature do not read the next few lines. The story of Keats and Fanny Brawne is a tale of almost unalloyed romantic tragedy. Keats left Hampstead to die of consumption in Italy at the age of 26, Fanny Brawne's mother burnt to death in the garden and Fanny remained in mourning for her poetic lover for six years. But it was here that Keats wrote his Ode to a Nightingale and Ode on a Grecian Urn, and the house now has a museum devoted to his memory.

At the bottom of Keats Grove turn right back into South End Road and you come to British Rail, Hampstead Heath. If you want to stop here, the train will take you to Kings Cross or you can turn right at the bottom (passing an extremely tempting cake shop). This is Pond Street. Behind you is the Railway Tavern if you require a little refreshment. Start walking up to the top passing the Royal Free Hospital on the left and the Roebuck Hotel on the right, which has the only cellar bar in Hampstead, as well as its beer garden, which is well worth a visit.

Turn left past the church at the end of Pond Street and walk down Rosslyn Hill to Belsize Park tube station.

8. Borough's Dickensian Roots

Highlights: See where Charles Dickens lived and where his father was imprisoned; admire London Bridge and Tower Bridge; shiver in the shadow of the Tower of London . . . and the possible presence of a friendly ghost.

Stations: Borough and Aldgate

Distance: 2 miles

"Debt, Devotion and Dickens". That would be a catchy name for a walk, and the route you will trace with me now takes in all that and, as they say – much, much more.

The Walk

For the first part come out of Borough Station and to your left is Sanctuary Street which leads into Lant Street. It was here that a very young Charles Dickens lodged as a young boy while his father languished in the local debtors' prison. Dickens described the street in 'Pickwick Papers' and in truth it is no less dreary a Dickensian scene now than it was then. Looking around this little cluster of streets, even the most unobservant of tourists will suspect that this part of London is closely associated with the great novelist, for if you look on the map, there is Little Dorritt Court, Copperfield Street, Pickwick Street, Dickens Square, Weller Street. No chance to forget just whose famous roots lie here! There's Disney Place and Disney Street – is this a town planner's attempt to immortalise the innumerable animated versions of a Christmas Carol?

This area also contains Mint Street, appropriately named (as you would guess) after a mint operating in the time of Henry VIII.

Kings Bench Prison

Money obviously played an important part in the lives of local residents (mainly because a high percentage of local residents round here were inextricably involved in the money business – either owing it, stealing it, imprisoning other people for it, or simply not having enough of it). Prior to 1842, when it was closed, this was the area of the "Liberty" of the King's Bench.

Now if you think that a modern open prison is lax, perhaps you should take a look at the conveniences provided in this institution (if you could pay for them of course!) The use of a coffee-house, two pubs, clean spring water and a market could be purchased from the governor for a proportion of the prisoner's indebtedness (a day pass could also be bought for 4s. 10d. (about 25p) for the first day, and 3s. 10d (about 20p) for ensuing days. Since it was reported that the "rules" or liberty at one point extended to the East Indies, this was exceptionally good value. In fact, conditions for those with resources were so good that prisoners transferred themselves to it from other parts of the country! Creditors might watch a debtor live in apparent luxury within the confines of the prison without being able to get hold of the money "owed". Of course for those without "resources" it was prison and pretty dreadful.

Do not confuse the Kings Bench Prison with the Marshalsea Prison, where Charles Dickens' father languished as a debtor which was described as "An old pile most dreadful to the view". Around the Prison, and Mint Street in the seventeenth and eighteenth centuries there also existed what amounted to a No-Man's-Land for criminals who had decided that they were beyond the law. Despite futile attempts to bring the process of law to this area, the population operated a rough and ready justice to bailiffs foolhardy enough to attempt to gain access. Some of the methods used to deter such men of authority included ducking them in an open sewer or making them kiss a brick dipped in the sewer or simply (and more hygieni-cally) being thoroughly soaked under a water pump.

Borough High Street

It would probably now be a good idea to look for some refreshment and Borough High Street has been famous for its pubs for hundreds of years. Set as it was on the approach to London Bridge, it was an obvious place for travellers to stop before entering the City. As always, publicans were keen to take advantage of the trade with the result that one satirist described it as "a continued ale-house, not a shop to be seen between red-lattice and red-lattice: no workers, but all drinkers". There still seems to be very few shops, but the workers appear to have overtaken the drinkers!

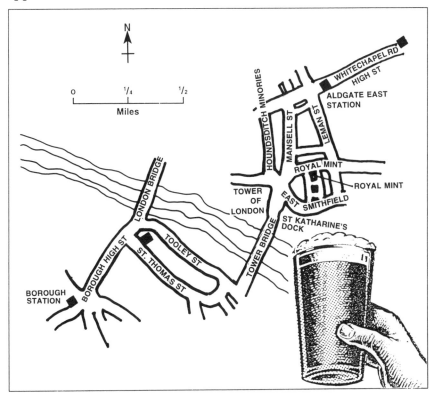

While we're talking about beer, it is probably worth mentioning the Hop wheeling and dealing which used to centre round this part of the world. Hops are a very important commodity for brewers and the uncertainty of the crop provided speculators with enormous potential for making (and losing) lots of money. Alas, no mobile phones in the early version of a modern futures exchange but the pubs provided an excellent (and appropriate) trading floor! The Hop Exchange stands as a monument to this early enterprise and though you can no longer gamble on the likelihood of a good harvest in the Southwark inns, you can drink the finished goods!

Unfortunately, all of the most famous inns have been pulled down. The names remain for some, like the Blue Eyed Maid on the right as you walk up, but for the most part you will have to shut your eyes and imagine what the High Street was like when Chaucer's Pilgrims gathered at the Tabard (commemorated in street names if nothing else since a Railway company decided to demolish it) to set out for the world's first recorded organised excursion. Talbot Yard is the site of Chaucer's Tabard Inn. Also disappeared is the White Hart (sited in the Yard named after it) where Jack Cade stopped before taking his Kentish rebels to London Bridge. It was one of Jack Cade's rebels, Jack Straw, who lent his name to the pub near Hampstead Heath.

The George

But one old inn does still exist to fire the imagination. The George. This is the last surviving galleried coaching inn, in the capital. Now preserved by the National Trust, the original sixteenth century inn was burnt down in the great fire in Southwark in the late seventeenth century, but appears to have been rebuilt as a replica of the original. Is this the first flowering of the modern drink industry's obsession with olde-worlde or was it simply cheaper not to have new plans drawn up?

Before permanent theatres were constructed in the late sixteenth century, performances by travelling companies would be held in the courtyard, watched either from the galleries or by the "groundlings". Prostitutes and pick-pockets would carry out their business while the audience enjoyed the performance (the weather no doubt in those idyllic days of Merrie Englande was a little more clement than it normally is these days for open air entertaiment).

Now owned by the National Trust, the pub is a remarkable monument to the simple tastes of Londoners' forbears. No cushions on the benches, but plenty of history, including a 1797 Act of Parliament clock (provided so that customers could avoid paying a tax on watches by taking advantage of a communal time piece) and Charles Dickens' life insurance policy, pledged behind the bar in exchange for a drink when he came in temporarily short of cash.

The fact that he never came back to claim it, says something either about his memory, or the quality of the service in those days!

Now drag yourself away from this pub and turn right out of George Inn Yard towards London Bridge and the river. Using the wonderful subway system come out in Tooley Street.

Tooley Street

Tooley Street was the home of " Three Tailors" who according to legend, despite being a very small sample, sent a petition to the House of Commons beginning "We the people of England". Equally worthy of note is the fact that Keats lived just off Tooley Street when he was a medical student nearby. Much more exciting and spectacular, however, is that it was also the scene of a huge fire in 1861 which caused around £2,000,000 worth of damage (a pretty hefty sum in those days – and indeed quite a lot now!) and provided a pleasant evening's entertainment for thousands of Londoners who thronged to watch it from every vantage point available, including church steeples, and even ironically the top of the Monument. The fire, which raged a quarter of a mile long was made even more of an attraction when a row of schooners, moored on the river, and loaded with tar and oil also caught fire giving the impression that the river itself was ablaze. One of the landmarks which was gutted in this fire was Hay's Wharf, the oldest Wharf in the Port of London. After the fire the Wharf went on to become the first to incorporate cold storage (enabling Londoners to enjoy New Zealand butter and cheese as early as 1867) Now completely refurbished to become quite a classy little shopping centre this is worth a look round. Refreshment is on hand both from the Balls Brother Wine Bars and Hays Galleria. The latter is a most extraordinary confection based on a Victorian Gin Palace meets David Livingstone theme. A frieze celebrates the travels of the head of the Horniman tea family whose collection of artifacts can be seen at the Horniman Museum in Forest Hill, London.

Also worth inspection is the centrepiece of a vast moving "Heath-Robinson" mechanical ship which appears to have been soldered together out of old bicycles. Hay's Wharf leads out onto the river and to HMS Belfast, largest cruiser ever built for the Royal Navy which is now permanently moored here as a tourist attraction and floating conference centre.

After Hay's Wharf go back onto Tooley Street and turn left. Make your way down to Horsleydown Road and to the Anchor Tap where this 200 year old pub is said to be haunted by a friendly ghost called "Charlie". One of the things it is said that Charlie does is move things like watches, hiding them for a few months until they are considered well and truly lost and then putting them somewhere unlikely, such as the airing cupboard. Obviously, drinking one's pint quickly is important here – before Charlie removes it!

Tower Bridge

We are now approaching Tower Bridge – that wonderful gothic pastiche which allegedly the Americans thought-they were buying when they paid their deposit on a particularly boring London Bridge. Opened in 1894, I think it's a wonderful example of pre-Disneyland architecture. It is of course not so much fun if you are stuck in a traffic jam on one of the occasions when they raise the bridge's centre sections.

St Katharine's Dock

On the other side of the bridge, past the Tower Hotel take a stroll round St Katharine's Dock. Before you get too excited about this new development it might be worth while remembering that this was originally a fine example of selfish and pig-headed development – albeit over 170 years ago. Practically an entire parish disappeared in 1825 including St Katharine's Hospital and a church. Over 11,000 people were turned out of their houses. There was not surprisingly a considerable amount of protest at the time, but money talked even louder then and the project went ahead. As if to emphasise the injustice of this mass eviction of the poor residents of St Katharine's, the earth removed went to help build fashionable Belgravia! For those who mourn such things this area is also the site of several breweries which fuelled Queen Elizabeth I's armies abroad.

Ironically, it was never a commercially successful venture and eventually the blitz destroyed what was left. The tourist development seems to have been a great deal more successful. Stop for a drink at the Dickens Inn which pretends to have a much greater age than it really possesses and have a look round at the collection of historic ships.

Coming out of St Katharine's Dock, cross over to the Minories. Of course on the left you can hardly miss The Tower of London, home to large numbers of unfortunate victims of rapidly changing political ideologies (being a member of the opposition was not a healthy occupation in Merrie Englande) and Tower Hill, where most of them and their heads parted company.

The Minories

Wrapping your scarf securely round your neck (no point in tempting fate!) head off down the Minories. It seems impossible to me that this place once boasted a farm where you could get milk fresh from the cows and a ditch so deep that men and horses could drown in it, but so it seems. After the cows moved out, the gunshops and armourers moved in and the offices have steadily taken over since then.

Continue down the Minories and you will get to Aldgate Station. If you want a last drink on the way home turn down Royal Mint Street passing the Royal Mint – now another "development" (our money is currently manufactured in Wales) – and turn up Leman Street. With the Sir Sydney Spenser on your left, you will see the Brown Bear, now a very respectable pub indeed, catering for city gentlemen. But according to at least one source, in days gone by it was a real den of iniquity – a "scene of nameless night orgies and murderous assaults". No doubt less fun these days, but the service is probably better!

Go out of the Brown Bear and turn right up Leman Street. Eventually you will find yourself on Whitechapel High Street and Aldgate East Station.

9. Roundabout Trafalgar Square

Highlights: Trafalgar Square, the National Gallery, Covent Garden, Lincoln's Inn and Carey Street. Visit London's oldest restaurant, a church "not much better than a barn" and the Museum of Freemasonry.

Stations: Trafalgar Square and Chancery Lane

Distance: 1½ miles

It was inevitable that sooner or later walking around London you would have to spend some time in Trafalgar Square. Ignore the tourists craning up at Nelson standing on top of his 145 foot high column (he's not going anywhere, you can look at him some other time). The Square has always been an open space, except once it boasted a huge variety of cookshops, and was called Porridge Island.

The Lions are quite interesting too, possibly because for a long time they were notable by their absence. Nelson arrived (by public subscription) on top of his column in 1843 – the lions were embarassingly delayed for another 25 years. If you want to look at "live" members of the animal kingdom, there's far more sense in paying close attention to the pigeons, who bear more resemblance to an airborne tank division than your normal run-of-the-mill feathered friends. Just watch them homing in on some well-meaning visitor who has been innocent enough to provide them with food.

If you happen to be around in the winter, at Christmas time you may be tempted to go down to the celebrations in Trafalgar Square on New Year's Eve.

The Walk

Leave the station and walk towards the National Gallery. Spare a glance for this fine building (remembering that in previous centuries, the space was occupied by a menagerie, a prisoner of war camp, stables and a public records office) which was once referred to as The National Cruet Set. With the gallery on your left-hand side walk towards the Strand and turn left in front of St Martin's in the Fields, the imposing church situated on the other side of the road. I find this church curious because, frankly, it has plummeted down the social scale in its very long history. Once called the Royal Parish Church, blue-blooded babies (including Charles II) have been christened here, and with a nice touch of irony, Nell Gwynne, his most famous mistress is buried here.

In its latter years, however, the crypt has become better known popularly for its soup kitchen for the London homeless, than for its illustrious bodies – even to the extent that Anneka Rice once did one of her famous "challenges" jobs for them.

The Church has also been witness to some non-religious visitors, such as the man who ran in on Good Friday 1687 with his sword drawn, pursued by bailiffs. There was also a creditor who came in wielding a pistol, shot one of the congregation and injured the preacher.

Having checked your credit references and ensured you are lucky enough not to need the ministrations of the good people of St Martins, you could pop into the Chandos which is just a little further down St Martin's Lane before you turn off into Chandos Street.

Maiden Lane

Now you may wish to take a small diversion here and just carry on a few steps beyond where we will eventually turn left and go down Maiden Lane. Despite its diminutive size this is one of those places which have been stuffed with names you should have heard of. Turner the artist, Marvell the poet, Voltaire the writer have all stayed here at some point. Queen Victoria's coach used to pass through here and of course this is where Rules Restaurant still provides meals and atmosphere to its customers. The restaurant is getting on for 300 years old (it's supposed to be the oldest one in London) and, yes, they've all been here – Dickens, Thackeray, H.G. Wells, and Edward VII. Actually, Edward VII used to come here with Lily Langtree, but to avoid comment, a special entrance was built for the happy couple so they did not have to go through the main restaurant.

However, back to our main route after this little diversion and left into Bedford Street. On the right-hand side you will be passing the offices of The Lady, the magazine where generations of infant aristocrats have advertised for young ladies to look after them. Inigo Place on the right leads you to St Pauls Church, Covent Garden. Inigo Jones, the architect responsible for the church was asked to produce something "not much better than a barn". If you have a chance look at the Church, it is rather more impressive than most barns you will see!

Further on up here we will pass Moss Bros on the corner of King Street and Bedford Street. This shop, is the place where you go if you are suddenly invited to an event rather grander than you are used to. Ascot, Henley, weddings, Royal Garden Parties, you can kit yourself out here. From humble beginnings in the beginning of the nineteenth century as second-hand clothes dealers the Moses (now Moss) family have developed a company without which there would be scarcely a top-hatted or tailed wedding in the land.

The Lamb and Flag

However, assuming that you have no great need of a full dress suit (or a ball gown) it would probably be more sensible to trot along a little way and take yourself up Floral Street which is just to the right. This street has been pedestrianised in that it is not a comfortable street to drive up. At this point, you're probably saying to yourself – "Funny kind of pub walk – where are the pubs?" Well, there is one just to the right of you through Lazenby Court in Rose Street, called The Lamb and Flag. Built in 1623, when gentrification had not reached this part of London (in fact judging by a contemporary report this particular place was full of gambling dens, drunks, and other undesirables). Bearing this in mind one can think that it was a tad reckless of John Dryden the Restoration poet to venture into this little alley. He found himself being beaten up by a gang of thugs (mistakenly) for writing scurrilous verses about one of Charles II's many mistresses. If you happen to be around on 19th December you may even be invited to Dryden Night which commemorates this dastardly but unsuccessful attempt on his life.

Fortunately for modern writers there appears to be no record of such violence against latter-day writers of less than flattering words about royal girl-friends! Who says we take these things more seriously now?

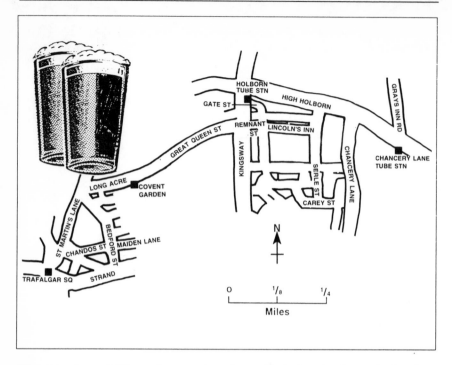

The Lamb and Flag also used to be called the Bucket of Blood, a name which refers to its association with prize-fighting rather than beating up wandering poet laureates. If you're interested in architectural details, the building is wooden framed with a Georgian facade.

Covent Garden

At the end of Floral Street you will come out into James Street, and if you want a more leisurely shop, a drink or something to eat there is Covent Garden in all its tourist glory. World famous, it hardly needs any introduction, except to say that like most places round here it no longer contains gambling dens, houses of ill-repute and other sinks of iniquity (or at least not to the naked eye). It was here that Fanny Hill, the notorious (fictional) heroine of a novel that was banned for 200 years, lived and it was here that the William Hickey (the non-fictional young man who has given his name to the newspaper gossip column) romped through his younger years, getting himself robbed, drunk and arrested in the eighteenth century. He later became a thoroughly respectable lawyer, probably almost as boring as the old men he had despised earlier on!

Assuming you have not been tempted to spend the rest of the day in Covent Garden you will eventually come in Long Acre where you will turn right and pass the Kemble's Head (or not, as it takes your fancy). This pub was another that once held a market licence (which meant that it could open at 5 a.m. for the Covent Garden market workers – for yes, this Market was once a real fruit and vegetable market).

Long Acre

Long Acre is not really a very exciting road, so perhaps that's why Samuel Pepys watched his coach being painted here one day for five hours – that must have been a really interesting diary entry!

At the end of Long Acre you will come into Great Queen Street which was once called the "first regular street in London" owing to its being entirely made up of brick houses! Quite something in 1612 when everything else was made of wood! Naturally, such a distinguished street has since that time been stuffed with famous names including all the usuals (James Boswell, William Blake, Richard Sheridan) plus Judge Jeffreys (the "Hanging Judge") and lots of others, of whom, if the truth be told I have never heard.

The large stone edifice taking up half of the right-hand side of Great Queen Street is Free Masons Hall, housing the Museum of Free Masonry, which is open to members of the public and free masons alike. If you need a quick pint there are many good pubs in and around Great Queen Street including The Pillars of Hercules.

However, at the bottom of Great Queen Street, you are about to embark on another adventure – you must cross Kingsway. I suggest you use the crossing by Holborn tube – you want to make the rest of the walk, don't you?

Having crossed Kingsway walk back up to where you would have been and turn into Remnant Street – possibly one of the most boring street names in London. Named as it is after Lord Remnant, barrister and MP for Holborn on the London County Council. Well, never mind, because Lincoln's Inn Fields, into which you are about to walk is considerably more entertaining (and there's a pub here as well!)

Lincoln's Inn Fields

This seemingly innocuous piece of land has a dark past, having witnessed at least sixteen executions during the reign of Good Queen Bess (during one of which the gentleman being hung drawn and quartered had the bad grace to survive his disembowellment – which even the Queen thought was a little much). A little later the place, while remaining a site for executions, also harboured all sorts of criminal types. Most recently it became a "tent city" for the homeless, but they seem to have been moved on now elsewhere. Undoubtedly the place looks tidier for it, but as a concerned Londoner, it would be better to know that they had been moved onto somewhere warm, rather than just another doorway.

However, the residents of Lincoln's Inn, being lawyers don't need to worry about such things, and on the left-hand side is the entrance to Lincoln's Inn itself. If you require some refreshment at this point, don't look for a pub called Lincoln's Inn. Lincoln's Inn is one of the Inns of court which provided rooms for student lawyers and continues to provide office accommodation for practising lawyers. There is in fact a pub tucked down right at the bottom of Gate Street, called the Ship Tavern, providing sustenance to lawyers and tourists alike.

As we move on, walk past Lincoln's Inn itself and turn right around the square. At the opposite corner to where you came in to the Fields you will find yourself in Serle Street (the name Serle seems to be associated with a long gone coffee-house, the haunt of lazy law students). (On the right, coming off of Serle Street is Portsmouth Street; if you really must, walk 200 yards and join the queue to visit the Old Curiosity Shop, allegedly the hero of Dickens tearjerker).

The Seven Stars

At the bottom of Serle Street turn left and you will find yourself in Carey Street (although not metaphorically we hope because I always think of Carey Street as being a polite way of saying "bankrupt" – since it is the traditional home of the Bankruptcy Court).

Here (at last) we come to another pub which is worth visiting or even staying in for some time! The Seven Stars, dating from 1602, perhaps named to celebrate the League of Seven Stars, in honour of visiting sailors from the Netherlands. It would be interesting to know whether the house was frequented by Dutchmen because they could get their favourite beer there – brewed as it was with new-fangled hops specially introduced less than a hundred years before for the Dutch merchants. Whatever the likelihood of this, it is certainly now full of solicitors, barristers and great gangs of tourists who think "British pubs are wonderful". The other interesting thing about this pub is the staircase which is boxed in, probably because it does not appear to go anywhere! Another piece of imaginative seventeenth-century building!

A little past the Seven Stars is the Silver Mousetrap, a jewellers who claim to have been founded in 1690.

Now walking straight down you will come to Chancery Lane. Turn left. There is not much, if anything left of what has been a City street since London's early mediaeval days, but continue until you come to High Holborn. Turn right and walk to Chancery Lane Tube Station. Don't go down the station yet. Just take a look at the famous Old Holborn buildings dating back in part to 1586 and immortalised on the Tobacco Tin carrying the same name. If you have a mind to, enter through the arch in the Old Holborn buildings and walk through to Staples Inn where you will find yourself back into the eighteenth century. Or, you might, since this is supposed to be a pub walk, go up Grays Inn Road to the corner of Theobalds Road and find one of the established brew pubs in London, the White Horse.

---

10. Moorgate to Islington

Highlights: Whitbread's HQ, the place where the balloon went up, the Eagle Taven (of nursery rhyme fame), Sadlers Wells, the Business Design Centre and a Saturday street market.

Stations: Moorgate, Highbury and Islington (BR)

Distance: 1½ miles

If the area around Moorgate looks a bit grim and cityfied now, just imagine it 500 years ago when Londoners would go through the gate to leave the city and enjoy the delights of the marshy moor which lay outside the city. Hence 'Moorgate'. On Finsbury Field every August, a mediaeval version of TV's "Gladiators" would take place. Tough men of the City would challenge the men from the "suburbs" to wrestle. Archers would compete in competitions. In the winter, citizens could divert themselves with ice-skating. Less wholesome pleasures could be taken at the brothels in this area some of which even catered for wives with absentee husbands (although the brothels were occasionally raided, resulting in considerable embarrassment for these "respectable" women"). Among the not-so-respectable women was a lady who traded from the aptly-named "Hand and Urinal" who claimed to be able to cure you of syphilis (and give you a quick beauty treatment into the bargain!).

The Walk

We start off this walk at Moorgate tube station. When you look at Finsbury Pavement now, it seems unlikely that there could ever have ever been such fun and games here. But for the thirsty. there was once even a working brewery just down the road in Chiswell

Street (on the left). Now the plush headquarters of Whitbread, the
national brewer, there was a time when the buildings here wafted
the aroma of boiling hops and malt into the city air, mingling with
the smell of the brewery draft horses in their stables (the horses have
since moved to Kent). I remember when a friend of mine was the
farrier to these mighty beasts and he was delighted to find that part
of his payment each week was an allowance of beer!

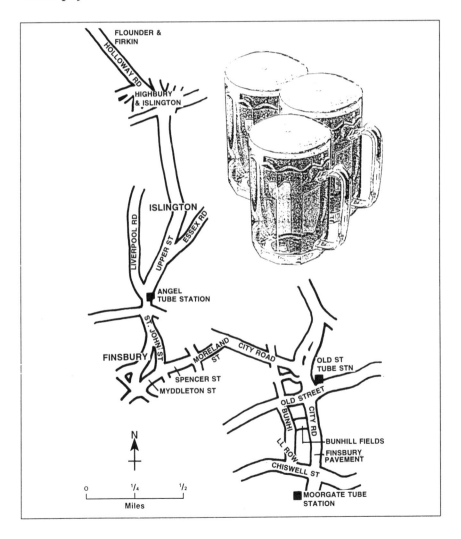

Honourable Artillery Company

As you go up City Road, there is the Honourable Artillery Company's barracks. As part of the Territorial Army, it is a volunteer force, but one which dates back to Henry VIII. With such former members as Wren, Pepys and Milton (who lived round the back in Bunhill Row and wrote Paradise Lost here) no doubt the despatches were beautifully written. The company also played host on this site to the first serious Cricket Match in the country, between Kent and All England in 1774. There had been a cricket club here since 1700, and the game attracted enormous crowds. There was no sexism in the game then and young women were welcomed as members. One other notable pastime which "took off" in England from behind these grim walls was the noble art of ballooning. The first ascent was watched by the Prince of Wales in 1783 and included among its passengers a dog, a cat and a pigeon (nobody has explained to me why the pigeon should bother with this uncertain form of transport!) The sport was soon a sensation, even to the extent that "balloon" hats became the rage for a short time with the most fashionable young ladies of the age.

Bunhill Fields

Further along the road, Bunhill Fields shelters such serious minds (and the bodies) of notable non-conformists such as William Blake (even by his time in the early nineteenth century there was very little "green and pleasant land" left in this part of the world), John Bunyan and Daniel Defoe. As well as these distinguished men under this ground also lie the bones cleared out from the Charnel House of St Pauls Cathedral in 1549. So do be careful where you walk! Spiritual and physical sustenance is available at the Artillery Arms opposite the cemetery.

Further along, walk under the subway at Old Street tube station and take the exit to City Road on the North Side (don't even think about crossing at ground level). We are now into what could be called "Londoners" London. It's not architecturally exciting, but people still live and work round here.

The Eagle

On the left-hand side of the road is Moorfields Eye Hospital, which was founded in 1805 (although it has occupied its present site for nearly 100 years) after troops returning from Egypt during the Napoleonic Wars came home suffering from trachoma and spread the disease in this country. A little further up City Road is Shepherdess Walk and the Eagle Pub, immortalised in the words of the song

"Up and Down City road
In and Out of the Eagle,
That's the way the money goes
Pop goes the Weasel"

The last line refers to the tailor having to pawn (pop) his iron (weasel) when money was short – from spending too much time in the Eagle! This pub is of course not the original Eagle, which was demolished in 1882 to make way (appropriately enough) for a Salvation Army Centre with barracks replacing the pub's bandstand. In its heyday, the first Eagle Tavern was a sight to behold with large grounds, an outdoor area for dancing (including fancy dress events which earned a rather seedy reputation) and a theatre inside for a range of treats which included everything from opera to variety acts. (Marie Lloyd apparently played here at the age of 14).

City Road

Having stopped at the Eagle Tavern for a quick recitation of the nursery rhyme come back onto City Road and you will be walking over the City Road Basin which is a branch of the Grand Union Canal which would take you all the way to Birmingham (if you weren't walking up towards the top end of City Road).

It is of course only sensible to advise walkers to mind the traffic but as you look up City Road bear in mind that 150 years ago this was the scene of furious races between rival horse-pulled omnibuses going at the breathtaking speed of 12 miles per hour. Sad to say this resulted in the death of at least one pedestrian. We are now going to

divert off the City Road, down Moreland Street, Spencer Street and through Myddleton Street. (For the London House of Correction see the comments in the walk around Clerkenwell Green).

New River Head

When you arrive at the Myddleton Street you will be in Roseberry Avenue. Turn right and you will come to an imposing set of buildings which belong to the Thames Water Authority. This is the New River Head. It is not just an imposing set of buildings, but it marks the first commercial attempt to do something about the chronic shortage of clean water in London. Since the early days, both Thames water and spring water were used (and of course in direct proportion to the lack of water, the number of complaints grew – although I bet no-one moaned when the water conduit in Cheapside ran wine to celebrate Henry VI's return from his coronation in Paris!). King James I shared the financial backing (and the profits) of the scheme with Sir Hugh Myddleton (whose statue we see later on) and water was brought all the way from Amwell in Hertfordshire through King James' own Theobald Park. There was an unpleasant moment when the King's horse slipped and threw his Majesty (head first) into the supply, but James was not called "The wisest fool in Christendom" for nothing. No doubt the thought of all the profit he was about to make from the water rates helped ease the pain of his watery fall! However, do not run away with the idea that this fresh new supply would have impressed today's environmental health experts. The New River had its fair share of "additives" in the shape of dead dogs, cats, rubbish and sewage. Perhaps a stop at the next pub for a bottle of guaranteed sanitised bubbly H_2O would be in order!

Sadlers Wells

As we walk further up Rosebery Avenue, our thoughts must turn to refreshment of the spirit rather than the flesh. For we are coming to Sadlers Wells, a theatre which is now synonymous with culture, opera and ballet. It was not always so. The site has sheltered a pickle factory, a skating rink and even a boxing arena. Would the polite audiences of today have wanted to see the "tumbling and dancing upon ropes and wires" or the "firing of pistols in the air" or even the "rolling of wheel barrows upon a wire" for these were the delights offered in the middle of the eighteenth century . Originally a side-show to a medicinal well, the original theatre became very popular, at one time even attracting the patronage of Royal Princesses and nobility. Apparently, Islington Spa as the well was originally called, was particularly favoured by hypochondriacs. For those who are feeling a little unwell during peformances you may be able to persuade the management to let you sip the reviving waters which are still hidden away at the back of the theatre. On the other hand you are probably safer with a gin and tonic!

Such notable figures as the famous clown Grimaldi and the actor Edmund Kean began their theatrical careers here, but unfortunately it must also be recorded that a rather tragic false fire alarm at the beginning of the nineteenth century ended in the deaths of 23 people. Behind the theatre is the Shakespeare's Head.

St Johns Street

More theatrical excitement awaits us as we walk up Rosebery Avenue and into St Johns Street, for we are coming to the Old Red Lion. This is a splendidly dishevelled pub with a theatre upstairs, one of the many which London offers to people who can either not afford, or who want a change from, the West End. Intimate and inescapably uncomfortable, these theatres are inexpensive and offer a dazzling variety of dramatic experience from Shakespeare to obscure modern drama. The companies who perform in these thea-tres tend to be young and working on the absolutely thinnest of shoestrings. I would advise you to pick up some of the leaflets in either the Red Lion or any of the other pub theatres on this walk – on at least one of these stages you will find something entertaining.

The Angel

As you continue up St Johns Street, you will come to a busy junction which marks The Angel, Islington. Ignore the Cooperative Bank at the ground floor and looking upwards you will see the dome of what was once a famous pub (don't let the fact that the present building was originally built as a tea shop put you off!). Once upon a time this was a main staging post into London and the Angel Inn entertained significant numbers of travellers for at least two hundred years. Livestock could also stop off here to be fattened up before their final, fatal, journey to Smithfield. Humans could find the place just as dangerous since armed escorts were offered to those journeying at night through dangerous Islington. Take a note of The Pied Bull just at the entrance to Liverpool Road if you like a good night out with extraordinarily loud music. Sir Walter Raleigh once lived on this site and supposedly entertained his Queen here but rather more quietly one supposes. The owners have changed the name to Power Haus – so don't say you weren't warned!

Continuing further up we will now come to Upper Street. On your left you will pass what was once the Royal Agricultural Hall but has now been revamped into the Business Design Centre. It is now a successful centre for business exhibitions and home of an annual art show. But in days gone by it was everything from a sports hall (bicycle races to showjumping), livestock shows (including Crufts!), concerts and military tournaments. We will draw a veil over its less glamorous era as a parcel sorting office! On the right is Camden Passage with the York pub which is a pleasant place to have a refreshing drink before you tackle the second half of the walk. One of the York's recent famous residents was the most enormous Alsation called Guinness. This dog was huge, and unsuspecting customers would look round to find him propped up on the bar next to them!

With or without the dog, Camden Passage is a wonderful place to wander round on a Saturday. The Bazaar and the antique stalls are great fun. You probably won't find a forgotten masterpiece there, but there's plenty of atmosphere and it's a good way to spend an afternoon! On the right as we walk up Upper Street there is a statue to the very same Hugh Myddleton, who helped bring clean(er) water to London, standing proud in Islington Green.

Upper Street

Perhaps now is the time to consider that although on this walk, we don't go "behind" Islington, it would be well worth a detour to walk round behind the shops of Upper Street to look at what was once a very genteel place to live. There are still plenty of fine eighteenth-century houses and squares left in Canonbury, which lies on the East side of Upper Street, to show how elegant it was here in days gone by. Over the last few decades the area has of course been "gentrified" greatly so that many of the houses have been restored. Among the people who have lived in the area is Kate Greenaway (Victorian painter and inspiration behind all those chubby, charming little girls with frilly pinafores and rosy cheeks).

But there are compensations to the loss of gentility and a thriving variety of pubs is one of them. To list all the pubs from now on would be pointless. There are plenty along with restaurants of every ethnic persuasion. But I must mention at least a couple of them beause they should not be missed. First of all there is the Kings Head in Upper Street, which houses what was London's first pub theatre. There is an abundance of pubs and small theatres around here – you probably noticed the Almeida as you walked past Almeida Street – that's another good place to stop for a glass of wine and a snack, particularly if you are going to the theatre there). The Kings Head normally has lunchtime shows as well as evening theatre so a good plan for this walk would be to aim to get there at about 1.00 pm. Don't be put off by the cash register behind the bar, which appears only to accept pre-decimal money. Unkind people say it's because the management were too mean to buy a new till but I think it's charming. They of course do accept normal currency! If you come back in the evening you can partake of a dinner as well as watching a first class performance. It has to be said that the food often doesn't achieve the same level of excellence as the acting, but the atmosphere is good and the meals are not expensive, so don't be put off.

Islington Town Hall is on the right and, if you peek in to look at the entrance hall, it is very impressive.

Continue walking past at least one terrace of pretty Victorian cottages.

We are now at the big roundabout which joins Upper Street to Holloway Road. On the opposite corner is The Hen and Chickens which is yet another pub theatre. At this point if you are tired perhaps it would be better to go into Highbury and Islington Station or if you have the energy you can continue up Holloway Road past the University of North London and Flounder and Firkin, which was one of the original Firkin pub-breweries from the 1980s and has now been absorbed into one of the National Breweries. Another short walk and you will find yourself at Holloway Tube Station.

11. Docklands

Highlights: Cable Street, where Fascists and Communists fought a pitched battle; Wapping, where pirates were executed and 'orrible murders committed; The Prospect of Whitby, where Pepys, Dickens and Turner had a jar or two.

Stations: Shadwell and Westferry (Docklands Light Railway)

Distance: 2½ miles

The extraordinary thing about this part of the world is that it changes literally from day to day.The work may not be as brutal or radical as it was a few years ago, and maybe the ratio of site to finished building has swung in favour of the completed article, but you still get a feeling of a Work in Progress rather than a settled, fixed environment. Maybe this is why it's interesting. And later on as you're walking around, if you wonder why the walk goes through the less charming and picturesque sights rather than along the Riverside Walk, it's because you can always go and look out on the Thames at any point during your amble (it's never far away), but you will miss the ghosts of the hard-drinking, hard-living sea-farers who used to live here if you only follow the river.

The Walk

We start off at Shadwell Station. Shadwell itself, although never what you might call a "smart" area, was home to many of the London-based sailors (including Captain Cook whose child was baptised at St Paul's Church which is a little further up the road in The Highway.)

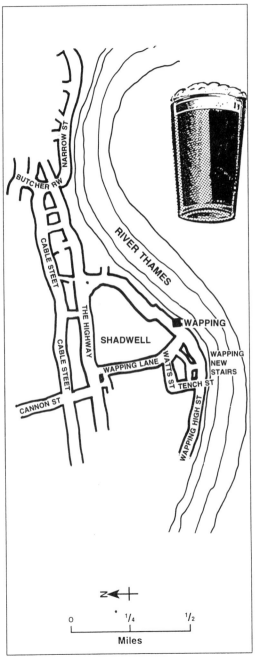

But we are beginning at Cable Street which is named (and it's obvious when you think of it) after the cables used by ships in days gone. Originally it was the length of a cable (600 ft) but it grew a bit over the years.

Quiet as it looks now this little bit of the East End has in its day seen some very fierce political activity. Cable Street itself saw a pitched battle between the Communists and the Fascists in the shape of Sir Oswald Mosley's Brown Shirts on a march. Not surprisingly, since the local population (particularly those coming from Whitechapel and Stepney) was predominantly Jewish, there was a flood of support for the left wingers (my father among them). They set up barricades in the road and eventually the march was stopped.

Now turn left at the top and into Cannon Street Road.

St George's in the East

Just around the corner is St George's in the East, a Hawksmoor Church which also saw duty as a centre for protest and insurrection, although in this case it seemed to take on a rather more irreverent manner (strange when you think the protests took place in a church!). Apparently, in the 1860s the local population took offence at a rather High Church vicar and yelling "No Popery!" they would disrupt church services every Sunday. They brought their dogs in, they threw orange peel and nuts at the Altar, they slammed doors, they let off fireworks. It no doubt enlivened the services and probably attracted a considerably enlarged congregation but of course the fun could not continue and the Vicar gave up.

I remember being taken there from my local Grammar school (Henry Raine, the founder had been buried there) and crowds of us staring at his grave on Founder's Day. Some of the more unfortunate ones being forced to wear early eighteenth-century clothing for the day as well. I don't know if this was intended to make us consider the emblems of mortality, but it succeeded in making the sixth formers who had to wear the costumes very uncomfortable and it gave the rest of us a day off afterwards! If we had known then how exciting the services in the Chuch had once been maybe we would have taken more interest!

The Highway

At the top of Cannon Street Road, turn left into the Highway. Be grateful you will not be spending much time on the Highway once known in more notorious times as Ratcliff Highway (and the scene of dreadful murders see below), and apparently the hangout for "loose damsels". No doubt the damsels could not negotiate the traffic these days. The first building Stow the sixteenth-century chronicler remembers, is a "fair free school" for sixty poor men's children. All this could be achieved on £50.00 per year including paying the schoolmaster and the usher. Alas, things have gone downhill considerably since then. In fairness he also remembered "Fayre hedges, long rowes of elme, and other trees" before the tenements appeared.

Wapping Lane

Crossing the Highway very carefully, you will come to Wapping Lane which featured a final episode in the appalling Ratcliff Highway Murders of 1811. After two sets of apparently motiveless multiple murders and another equally brutal murder in the King's Arms pub in Wapping Lane (which has now disappeared), a sailor was eventually arrested who hung himself on the night of his arrest. Justice was a brutal occupation in those days, however. Paying absolutely no heed to good taste, the body of the suicide was carried past the site of the murders, had a stake driven through its heart and then was unceremoniously dumped in a specially dug pit in Cannon Street Road.

Almost immediately in Wapping Lane you will find yourself walking past Tobacco Dock, one of the new Docklands improvements. Now a shopping and business centre it sports a couple of boats outside and if you want to, you can walk all the way to Shadwell Basin along the ornamental canal. On the other hand, you can keep on with this walk!

Turners Old Star

Turn right into Watts Street and you will come upon a little city pub which has an interesting (possible) history. This is Turners Old Star, which, it is claimed, was run by the painter Turner and his mistress (Turner for the purpose adopting an assumed name.) I do recall local historians demanding some documentary evidence for this claim, and I am not sure if any was forthcoming, but who cares – it's a good story.

Out of the pub turn left into Tench Street past The Barley Mow and an old school house which is in the process of being done up (or was, as this book was being written) and then turn left at the bottom into Wapping High Street.

This road was once a centre for sailors' entertainment and home to thirty-six taverns. Around here was the traditional place for "hanging Pirates and sea rovers at the low water mark, and there to remain till three tides had overflowed them". It has also charmingly been called

- "a continual street or filthy strait passage."

To the right is the Town of Ramsgate. The pub gains its present name from the Ramsgate fishermen who would come up (before the days of juggernauts and goods trains) to sell the catch for market. The pub has a more sinister history. It is the place where Judge Jeffreys, the infamous "hanging judge" who was attempting to escape to Hamburg (his reign of terror being over, he had now become a fugitive) was captured. He thought he was safe in Wapping (never the haunt of the upper ranks of society – at least not when they wanted to be recognised!) disguised as a sailor. Unfortunately, he happened to look up over his beer while sitting in this pub (then called The Red Cow) and of all people, who should he see but a lawyer he had once insulted in court. A swift removal to the Tower of London was effected and the Judge later died from a long and painful illness.

Wapping New Stairs

You will now pass Wapping New Stairs which used to serve as a spot for the execution of pirates (note that the local public house is named the Captain Kidd in "honour" of this gamekeeper-turned-poacher who was originally hired to round up the pirates. The temptation to join them was too much and he met his end here at Execution Dock as it used to be called).

Continue walking down Wapping High Street and take note of the wharves as you pass them, Swan Wharf, King Henry's Wharves, Gun Wharves, all tell the tale of more prosperous days for the area when this street swarmed with sailors and dockers, when there were dozens of pubs (and brothels) down here.

The Prospect of Whitby

As you walk along Wapping High Street, you will see glimpses of the river through the high wharf buildings – there is access to the Riverside Walkway where you can enjoy a stroll down by the Thames. But before you do that, you may prefer to seek out a pub well-known to tourists throughout the world – The Prospect of Whitby. Built in the time of Henry VIII, Samuel Pepys used to drink in this pub and in commemoration of the great man the Ancient Society of Pepys meets here. Naturally other notable drinkers of the arts world (Dickens, Turner) also used to come down here and it is said that it is here that the fuchsia first found its way into Britain through a deal done in this pub. The Prospect was once known as The Devil's Tavern (no need for an explanation I think!) and it was lucky for the owners that a boat called The Prospect from Whitby moored nearby attracting attention and giving them an excuse to change the name.

Highway to Limehouse

Coming out of the Prospect keep walking and you will eventually find yourself in Glamis Road which will take you past the Shadwell Basin Project, you will be able to see Canary Wharf in the distance (that huge tower block with the pyramid on top – which I find rather attractive, but I think I'm in the minority). This will take you briefly out onto the Highway once the centre of every conceivable vice (and a fair few that most people would never dream of). It might look like any old thoroughfare now but in days gone by there were opium dens, random knifings, dead bodies lying around with of course the mandatory desperadoes with knives stuck in their belts. Definitely not a place to spend a quiet afternoon or evening! We are coming up to a small group of charming pubs – hurry along and turn right down Narrow Street. This is now Limehouse, named after the Lime Kilns which used to abound. Just along the road in Narrow Street you will first come to The Barley Mow, which is a converted Lock Keeper's cottage. This cannot claim any real historical associations, but it has a charming terrace overlooking the Thames (the charm is greatly improved at high tide!) and is well worth a visit. Further along the road is The Grapes, renowned for its fish menu (the restaurant is tiny – it really is sensible to book in advance if you want to eat here). It is claimed that the pub is the basis for The Six Jolly Fellowship Porters in Dickens' Our Mutual Friend. All I can say is that it is not the only pub which claims this honour, but since I have no proof that it isn't, why not?

A little further up, there is another pub, which although making no claim to historic associations, is probably the most interestingly named. It's called The House They Left Behind – and that is exactly what they did. When they redeveloped the area a few decades ago, the pub earned itself a reprieve and so it remains – left behind.

The rest of the walk will take you further along Narrow Street until you come to Limehouse Causeway and the Docklands Light Railway, and home.

12. Piccadilly Circus to World's End

Highlights: from Piccadilly to Pall Mall, past the site of a leper hospital, to Hyde Park Corner and Berkeley Square. Go shopping along The Kings Road and finish at The World's End.

Stations: Piccadilly Circus and Fulham Broadway

Distance: 4¼ miles

It would be nice to say that some of the original houses built around here by Henry Jermyn were still here, but one must tell the truth and admit that they have all gone. Henry would probably have approved of the extraordinarily high class (and high priced) establishments to be found here, including somewhere not to stop for a snack if you're working to a tight budget – A L'Ecu de France, the legendary and expensive restaurant!

The Walk

Out of Picadilly Circus, turn down Piccadilly and into Jermyn Street. Then cross the road to Bolton Street (once the most westerly street in London). Henry James lived here. Turn left into Duke Street where you will see the Chequers which stands on what has been the site of a pub since 1732. Carry on down St James Row and turn right into King Street.

King Street

It's a shame but this is another street that has lost its original

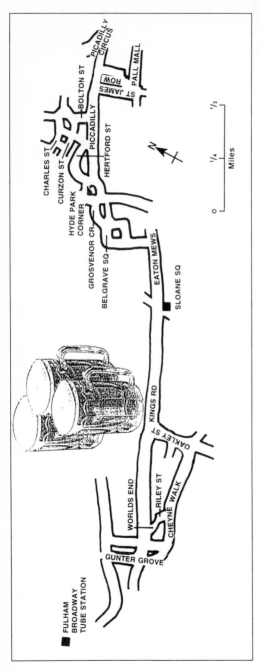

buildings, like the Feathers pub and Nerot's Hotel where Lord Nelson stayed when he was still a mere admiral and then later when he had been made a Lord. He met Lady Nelson on his return from the Battle of the Nile (one of the few places where the great sailor seems to have met his own wife rather than Lord Hamilton's). He also stayed there after he had understandably upset his wife over the lovely Emma H. Apparently, the food in this fine establishment was excellent, although one guest complained that he "nearly died" of it. St James Theatre replaced the hotel in 1835 and disappeared in 1959 having seen the first nights of such plays as "The Importance of Being Earnest". Lord Olivier (who had once unsuccessfully leased the theatre) and his then wife Vivien Leigh's protest at its demolition is recorded in their sculpted portraits on the wall at numbers 23 and 24.

Also disappeared (so far as one can tell) are the very

expensive courtesans who used to ply their trade for the rich residents and visitors. The brothels were known as "nunneries", the madames were referred to as "Abbesses" although presumably their habits were of a kind unknown in more orthodox religious establishments.

But of course there is a pub which is of greater interest (since you can still drink in there!) and it seems that the Golden Lion public house may well have had a presence in this street since the seventeenth century for an early map shows Crown Passage as "Golden Lion Court" by 1732. The present "Golden Lion" stands on a site occupied since 1762 but unfortunately the building itself, despite its strenuous attempts to show otherwise, is only late Victorian.

Then left into Crown Passage which is now occupied by the Red Lion. It is claimed to be one of the oldest licensed houses in the West End. The pub is just an orange throw from St James' Palace so it is hardly surprising that the rumour is that Charles II and Nell Gwynne are said to have met here. Try to forget that the pub and its environs stands on the site of a hospital for "leprous maidens" and think instead of the secret tunnel which reputedly runs from Crown passage to St James Palace down which (it is said) Henry VIII would escape from Ann Boleyn when her charms began to pall. It is also said that this was the site of the last duel in England. It is further rumoured that Texas had its embassy here.

Pall Mall

Now turn into Pall Mall which was a new road built to spare Charles II and his friends from the traffic disturbance of the old road which was too near their Pell Mell alley in the grounds of St James Palace. No doubt anyone else in the kingdom would have had to find somewhere else to play. But of course, if it's the King's highway he can put it where he likes! It was here that Charles could be seen talking to Nell Gwynne, whom he had thoughtfully placed in the house next door to the palace.

Piccadilly

Go right up St James Street, left into Piccadilly and then at Green Park cross to Bolton Street. The naming of Piccadilly is interesting since it shows once again how some London names are generated in the most bizarre fashion. A piccadill was originally a high ruffed collar and the area owes its name to the success of one Robert Baker who having made his fortune from this item of clothing bought himself a bit of land in the area. The house was jokingly dubbed "Piccadilly Hall" and so the name stuck – to the eternal irritation of people who can never remember how many c's, d's and l's you need to spell it correctly!

At the top right, turn into Fitzmaurice Place crossing Curzon Street and then turn left into Charles Street.

The Running Footman

Here at the corner of Hay's Mews is the "I am the only Running Footman". In itself a pleasant enough pub, the name over the door deserves an explanation. As you would expect, the story is bizarre. Originally called the Running Horse, in 1810 the 4th Duke of Queensbury, a fabulously wealthy and typically eccentric member of the English aristocracy discovered that his footman was a potential Olympic standard marathon runner (except of course they didn't have the Olympics, or even marathons, so he had to be content with racing his chap against other eccentric noblemen's footmen). He could apparently run for seven miles per hour in front of the Duke's carriage (not in slinky Lycra shorts either – his running gear was full livery – powdered wig, brocade jacket, stockings, buckled shoes etc. plus a special staff containing a refreshing mixture of wine and egg white – would the international athletics authorities have considered this an illegal substance?). Since at that speed he could also apparently pay tolls, carry lights at night and presumably help his master out of his vehicle, this was no mean feat – and it was with great pride that the Duke pinned up a sign outside the pub proclaiming "I am the only running footman" which also laid claim to being the longest sign of any London pub.

Shepherd Market

But this is a walk so do not fear, no running is expected of you. We will now turn south again to have a peek at Shepherd Market. Turn left down Queen Street cross Curzon Street and then through the covered alley at no 47. This was the very heart of Mayfair and the celebrations from which the district took its name. Please dismiss any romantic notions of shepherds and shepherdesses here, the place is actually named after the architect, Edward Shepherd, and the covered market he built in 1735. The fair that this attractive little warren of buildings replaced was eventually suppressed at the end of the eighteenth century, having given local residents an annual 15 days of abandoned fun (or abandoned dissolution, depending on how you looked at it!) from 1st May. In Hertford Street is the Shepherd's Tavern, which gained some fame during World War II as the accepted rendezvous for RAF aircrew. Airmen would leave their pewter tankards behind the bar ready for their safe return from flying missions. The Battle of Britain saw scores being kept of planes shot down on either side and no doubt the pewter mugs filled with joy (and ale) to cheer the RAF's own successes.

Hyde Park Corner

Walk along Hertford Street and you will come to Park Lane. On Hyde Park Corner you may want to go into Apsley House which was given to the Duke of Wellington in 1820 by a grateful nation. This piece of land seems to have a history of being given away as a reward for bravery – the original house was built on an apple stall given by George II to an old soldier who had served his country well. Since the builder, Lord Apsley, actually had to buy the apple seller out, it is only to be hoped that the man got a good price for it – though probably nowhere near as much as the land is worth today!

Berkeley Square

Cross under Hyde Park Corner, into Grosvenor Crescent and Belgrave Square. Despite its rather grand appearance the history of Belgravia is rather dull, perhaps only given even a spark of interest by its proximity to the former Lock Hospital, built to cater for "females suffering from disorders contracted from a vicious course of life". It is really rather a shame because before the building up of this area was started in the early nineteenth century it sounded much more exciting. Londoners kept themselves entertained while it was still countryside here with duck shooting, bull-baiting and cock-fighting. At night danger lurked, and murders, duels, highwaymen and general bad deeds abounded. But in daylight it, at least, looked and smelled pleasant – the fields provided Jonathon Swift with the sweet perfume of "flowery meads" and haymaking (while also noting that the girls involving in harvesting were not particularly attractive). One hundred and fifty years later it was not so agreeable – Belgrave Square was eventually built over a sewer which "abounded in the foulest deposits . . . emitting the most disgusting effluvium." Being bitten by a rat was not an uncommon hazard of living in this fashionable part of London and pre-public health and hygiene typhus was a fact of life for the wealthy inhabitants. No doubt when the wind was in the right direction the smell was enriched by the aroma from Tattersall's equine sale rooms at Hyde Park Corner and the innumerable mews and stablings nearby.

Eaton Mews

Keep walking and eventually your patience will be rewarded with a delightful pub called the Antelope which is reached by going along Belgrave Place and right along Eaton Mews. According to the brewers the pub was built in 1780 when it was still a very rural area with tea huts and rustic buildings all around. The first serious property development was in 1826 when houses were put up in Eaton Square. This little pub has retained its original charm and even some of its original woodwork. Naturally, the clientele has changed in the last 170 years, but it probably still has its fair share of staff who work in the grand houses nearby. At one point it was common to see the senior servants such as butlers and valets drinking in the private bar, while the juniors drank in the tap-room.

Upstairs meals are served in a little dining room. Prices have gone up since the days when you could get a "luncheon of onion soup, jugged hare and rhubarb tart for 6s. 6d (about 33p; cream 1/- extra) or a dinner for 7s. 6d (37.5p) but it is still a darn sight cheaper than eating in most other places in Belgravia! Obviously a good place to charge your batteries before tackling the excitement of the next part of the walk – Chelsea.

Chelsea and The Kings Road

Come out of Eaton Terrace, right along Cliveden Place and you will very soon find yourself in Sloane Square. Turn left out of Cliveden Place past the Royal Court Theatre and then continue straight past John Lewis and you are now in The Kings Road. If you are intending to stop in all the bars along the way you probably won't make it to the end so may I suggest a few which are worth stopping at (mainly because you can't go home without having been in them.) If you are genuinely interested in commercial trends the Kings Road is still invaluable, because it is here that people try out new ideas for bars and eating places. Perhaps it isn't quite as wild as it was in the "Swinging Sixties" (for it was here that the whackiest and wierdest boutiques rapidly opened and closed like the delicate little flowers they were) but it is still vibrant and busy and the shops are interesting. On a fine day there is still an element of a fashion parade up and down and if you must just watch the world go by, there are certainly few more entertaining worlds to watch.

The Six Bells (originally the Chelsea Artists Pub) 195 Kings Road haunt of artists and others such as J.M.W. Turner and Rossetti, Jacob Epstein, J.M. Whistler, Augustus John, Thomas Carlyle and Dylan Thomas.

The Chelsea Potter, 119 Kings Road, 100 yards from the Town Hall and the Lord Nelson, 200 Kings Road are both pubs worth looking into.

Turn left down Oakley Street to the Phene Arms (Thomas Carlyle lived in nearby Cheyne Row)

Cheyne Walk

Turn right along Cheyne Walk. As you would expect from such an attractive and elegantly appointed road such as Cheyne Walk its history is positively stuffed full of famous people from George Eliot to Lloyd George. Famous people are fairly dull when they are at home, but if the evidence from an establishment in Cheyne Walk is anything to go by, combining several famous poets in one house at least upsets the neighbours. It was actually Dante Gabriel Rossetti's fault when he shared number 16 with his friends Algernon Swinburne and George Meredith. Rossetti was fond of peacocks (everyone has their weaknesses) but unfortunately the birds made such a racket that now it is written into leases that new residents are not allowed to keep them. Do you think they would object to Minah Birds, Cockerels or Parrots?

Further up Cheyne Walk you will come to Danvers Street and Crosby Hall. Crosby Hall actually shouldn't be there – it was moved from Bishopsgate to Chelsea earlier this century. But it had some rather interesting previous owners (not the first occupant who was just a very rich grocer) including Richard III (the King who is accused of murdering the Princes in the Tower) and Sir Thomas More (who was himself beheaded by the Tower). Sir Thomas More once owned the land on which Crosby Hall now stands and wrote a history of King Richard III, but I think that is just a happy coincidence.

Danvers Street itself is remarkable (well I think so) for having been the home of the austere Dr Jonathon Swift and the place from where he wrote part of his "Journal to Stella" – a collection of letters written to a lady whom he never married (they say) but with whom he conducted a platonic relationship for thirty years. What is probably just as interesting (and certainly makes better gossip) was that he was also conducting a (supposedly) platonic relationship with his pretty young neighbour who later followed him to Ireland and possibly died of (maybe) unrequited love for him. As you can see there are a lot of "maybes" about this story but I think it's a jolly good one! What passions seethed under those powdered wigs!

Worlds End

Right up Riley Street and into Worlds End at the end of which you will find The World's End Inn, an establishment known since the days of Charles II as a good place to go for assignations, (or the after-effects thereof – I did read somewhere that Pepys came here to recover from an unhappy love-affair!) The current pub was built in this century, but no doubt not much has changed in the overall preoccupations of the customers! After the pub, turn left and then right up Gunter Grove which will eventually lead you to Fulham Broadway tube station.

13. St Pauls

Highlights: Cheapside, where fast food took off; Bow Church, possibly the unluckiest City Church; Bread Street, where Milton was born; views of the Mansion House, the Royal Exchange and the only inn to escape the Great Fire of London.

Stations: St Pauls and London Bridge

Distance: 1½ miles

I make no apologies. This is one of those walks around London that everybody does – because it's one of those areas which has been consistently seedy and therefore interesting for hundreds of years. Not surprisingly, the pubs here are full of other people drinking in great gulps of histórical presence – but that probably also hasn't changed for hundreds of years. William Shakespeare, Dr Johnson, Christopher Wren, Samuel Pepys, they are all remembered here.

The Walk

Come out of St Paul's and walk down Cheapside. Look at the shops because traditionally this was a great shopping street (the derivation comes from 'Chepe' – an early English word for market) and John Stow, one of the earliest enthusiastic London Tour Guide authors (and a contemporary of Shakespeare), describes Cheapside as "worthily called the Beauty of London". Well, obviously it's changed a bit since then but this street was one of the main processional routes through the city and the water conduits ran wine when the City Fathers thought a particular celebration merited it. One me-diaeval writer surely would not have agreed with this generosity when he complained of the "immoderate quaffing among the foolish sort ... ". He had obviously been in the City pubs after a particularly good day on the Foreign Exchange market! The sandwich bars are also here in good company – in earlier centuries "cooks cried hot ribs of beef roasted, pies well-baked and other victuals" Obviously fast food is not something invented recently.

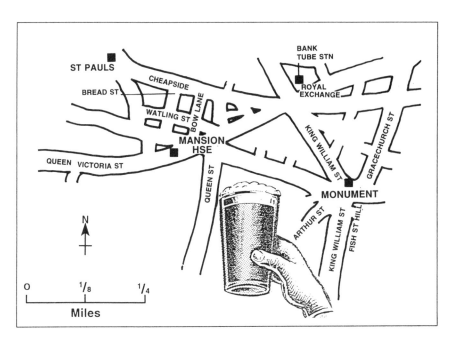

Bow Churchyard

Turn right down Bow Lane, and past Bow Churchyard. It was here that Boswell bought himself a whole package of children's books to help him recall his youth – before it became a mis-spent one! You probably have no need to walk carefully nowadays, but it must be admitted that this particular City church seems to have gained itself a reputation for disaster – for instance the roof came off in a storm, with "some persons slain" (presumably when the four 26 foot-long rafters fell on them); another time the tower collapsed killing 20 people and there was also a murder in the church itself. There might also have been fatalities if Queen Philippa, wife of Edward III, had not managed to persuade her husband not to punish the builders when the stand she and her ladies were sitting in collapsed. I don't know whether being a Cockney is lucky or not (although as a native of Whitechapel I am supposed to be one) but it is within the sound of the bells of this church that a true Cockney is born. The curfew was rung from them many years ago. These days the City after dark has once more reverted to the empty streets of a curfew but only because everybody has rushed home to watch the Australian soaps on TV. Continue past the Bow Wine Vaults carefully avoiding ladders, black cats, single magpies and other bad omens. (It is purely coincidence that Walk 13 includes the unluckiest church in London. Or is it?)

Williamsons Tavern

You will shortly come to a tiny yard called Groveland Court. It doesn't look particularly prepossessing, but right at the bottom is Williamsons Tavern, said to be the true centre of the City of London and an institution which has highest connections in the hospitality industry. The building which dates from the seventeenth century is on a Roman site and was once the official residence of the Lord Mayors of London. In this capacity the place played host to William III and Mary. The service must have been good because the wrought iron gates which front the pub were left, so to speak, as a tip from the Royal couple. No doubt in an effort to retain this kind of high class clientele, when Robert Williamson in 1739 decided to turn the place into a hotel, the house rules seems to have been remarkably strict (there was no licence to sell alcohol until 1851). Despite this, the place remained popular, even though the Victorian era brought even stricter rules, such as the enforced ban on anything but religious literature on Sunday.

But perhaps they thought inflammatory reading would be a fire hazard and the management worried about things like this – guests were not allowed to use matches to light their pipes. The ceilings were made of white cotton fabric pinned to the rafters – though why in such an inflammable atmosphere the management allowed pipes I cannot imagine! Since most bedrooms each held three or four beds, the prospect of all these pipe smoking guests in such close proximity to each other seems to me to constitute more of a pollution problem than a fire risk! There is also rumoured to be a ghost on the premises. Even fairly recently there was an incident where a constable patrolling the court stumbled as if he had been pushed from behind and cracked his head – the ghost was most likely simply emptying his pipe on the poor PC!

Bread Street

If you walk a little further down and turn right into Watling Street you will come to the Old Watling. But first glance down Bread Street. Although there is little left of the original street after the bombs of the second world war, it has an interesting history. John Milton was born down here and as you can tell by the name it is the site of the Bread Market (bakers were not allowed to sell bread anywhere else in the City but in an assigned market place.) In the true spirit of mediaeval fair play, tradesmen such as bakers who did not adhere to accepted standards of weights and measures received their just reward and would be "drawn on a hurdle through the streets of this city" with a "fool's hood on his head and loaves of bread about his neck ". A sliced loaf may always weigh the correct amount but does not carry the prospect of half so much entertainment value.

The Old Watling

But think of happier things because you are about to visit The Old Watling, built after the Great Fire of London – it dates itself from 1666. (This pub is also rumoured to be another one built by Sir Christopher Wren to give shelter and refreshments to his workforce – no wonder it took so long to finish St Pauls; the builders were in a permanent state of befuddlement!) It is also claimed that the pub served as an office for Sir Christopher (surrounded by his drunken workforce? The filing must have been interesting.) But for whatever purpose the place was built, it is supposed to incorporate some of the original materials, and it is interesting architecturally because the single bar arrangement is not because of the brewers going for greater square footage for drinking space, but is original. Of the three large beams in the bar, one takes the entire strain of the building – but have no worries. It "has been tested" to show that it will continue, happily, to take the strain for the next 1000 years. What is probably just as interesting is that the pub's ancient licence (now thankfully abandoned!) stipulated that customers would have to order a set meal before they could have their drink.

Turn left into Queen Victoria Street past Sweetings Oyster Bar which is on the corner of Queen Street and soon we will pass St Mary Aldermary. This unfortunate church has also been subject to various continuous rebuilding since the sixteenth century (it was damaged in the Great Fire and World War II.) The Victorians, however, may have been the most thoughtless when they restored it for no particular reason in the 1860s – removing most of the seventeenth-century woodwork in the process.

Walk past the Roman Temple of Mithras which was excavated in 1954 (its treasures are held in the Museum of London if you have a mind to see them) and cast your eyes (or even your feet) down Bucklersbury where you will see the Old City Shades.

We will next go back onto Poultry (named as you would expect after the poulterers who had originally carried on their trade here but had already moved on by the early seventeenth century). But it was also famous before the Great Fire of London for the number of inns and for one of the prisons belonging to the Sherriff of London (which Stow says had been there "time out of mind"). Perhaps it was the ancient facilities of this place which gave rise to the smell of "tobacco, foul feet, dirty shirts, stinking braths and unclean carcases". Or was that just the smell of the customers in the taverns?

Mansion House and Royal Exchange

We have come this way, I must admit, so that you can have a sight of the Mansion House which the Lord Mayor moved into in 1752 after 82 years of discussion. The building was rather inauspiciously, I think, built on the site of an area well-known as the meeting place of "sexual deviants". The building cost over £70,000 and was paid for out of fines on the Aldermen (a pretty fair rating system most Council Tax payers would reckon!) At one time this was a rather grander building with a large superstructure. Locals unkindly referred to it as the Mare's Nest and the offending extra bits were removed in 1840. Next to it the Royal Exchange (now an insurance office) stands on the site of what may have been England's very first shopping centre. Right from the sixteenth century the place was frequented by "Ratcatchers, Dog sellers and Courtesans" (rather a curious combination of clientele!) and attracted people who had nothing better to do than "curse and swear to the annoyance and grief of the inhabitants and passers-by" (shopping centres do not change you see), and shopaholics who could pop into any one of the

160 shops. You could probably get anything you wanted here – glass eyes, ivory teeth, corn plasters, spectacles. You could also be fairly sure of "a good time" since when it re-opened after the Great Fire it was considered just right for assignations. Prostitutes would make themselves available during opening hours and brothels abounded all around the area. It was obviously not a place for the most discerning of would-be lovers, since, you met an even better class of lover in the Strand (and apparently you got an even better class of assignee here than in St James Park). But it was a great place for tourists and for those who had a few hours to idle away. This included Boswell who once walked from St Paul's to the Royal Exchange, and "back again, taking the different sides of the street" eating a penny Twelfth-cake (all sugared over) at every shop where I could get it." and then "dined comfortably" at the other end of Cheapside. What a splendid appetite!

But now we have to work up an appetite like Boswells so we must carry on down King William Street looking up at the Monument as you go. If you're feeling energetic, by all means climb it, but don't, like Boswell, get frightened when you are half way up. He "despised" himself for his timidity and did not appear to enjoy it when he actually made it to the top since he said "it was horrid" and he "shuddered as every waggon passed down Gracechurch Street, dreaded that the shaking of the earth would make the tremendous pile tumble to the foundation." He restrained himself and did not add to the six suicides who have thrown themselves from its 202 ft. There is now a cage to prevent any more tragedies. Dickens, who was obviously a far more sensible fellow comments "It's worth twice the money to stay below". As most people know, the Monument was built to commemorate the Great Fire of London in 1666 and "to preserve the memory of this dreadful Visitation".

Walk along past Post Office Court down Abchurch Lane (just think, in this road many years ago you could have had a choice of a famous French eating house or visiting the man who invented a cure for worms – on second thoughts, don't think of this, there's a good pub coming up soon!)

Old Wine Shades

Down Martin Lane past the Old Wine Shades – "The only city tavern to escape the Great Fire" it says and claims to be the oldest wine house in the City. It may well be since it has 1663 emblazoned on a lead cistern in the garret. As "Shades" it is well named – inside does have the feeling of being built inside a room-sized pair of sunglasses.

In 1900 it was described as being so dim that the visitor's eyes actually needed time to get accustomed to the gloom. It retains its air of Victoriana although the tables are no longer "black with age". Now that it is of course cleaner, and escaped demolition in 1972 it will probably be with us for some time. The term "shades" was often used to describe drinking places a couple of centuries ago, particularly if they were in cellars or shaded from the sun – as this one obviously is.

London Bridge

Into Arthur Street and you will walk past The Porters Lodge which deserves merit for not even pretending to be old. We are now in Lower Thames Street and we're going to turn left now opposite the Parish Church of St Magnus the Martyr. Up Fish Street Hill – now you can look back up at the Monument and regret not walking up it (or walking up it depending on the state of your health). We're going to continue up Monument street and walk over London Bridge. This is the replacement for the London Bridge which has been shipped to Arizona. But there have been lots of London Bridges (five in all). They burnt down, fell down (as it says in the nursery rhyme) and one even got blown away; but I personally think the most interesting London Bridge story is the one where it gets towed away – a warning that you can't even park a bridge in London? Sadly no, just a Norwegian King helping our own Ethelred the Unready to get rid of some Danes (personally I like to think he ran out of 20 groat pieces – but of course that's just fantasy!)

If you look over the left-hand side of the now securely fastened London Bridge you can see Tower Bridge and HMS Belfast. Save those for another walk. But you can also see Canary Wharf, perhaps the most talked about building in recent years. I happen to like it, but of course I know nothing about architecture so make up your own mind! On the right-hand side of the bridge you can see St Pauls, St Brides and the Post Office Tower. And underneath, the Thames just rolls along quite indifferent to what you think about it. In days gone by, the old bridge used to slow the river flow down so that in a very cold winter it would freeze over and Frost Fairs were held on the ice where enterprising Londoners could make money roasting oxen, printing commemorative and personalised posters and other delights.

As you leave the bridge you pass out from under the protection of the City's Griffins and into the Borough of Southwark. If you think you've had enough walking for the time being London Bridge Station is conveniently situated nearby – but please use the underpass!

14. Over London Bridge

Highlights: Southwark and its Cathedral, Bankside and (its previous) brothels, the site of the oldest City inn, high and low cultural connections from Shakespeare (including the site of the Globe Theatre) to bull-baiting and prize-fighting.

Stations: London Bridge and Blackfriars

Distance: 2 miles

Imagine it's an afternoon in Shakespearean London. You're a young man at a loose end, looking for something to do and somewhere to show off a new set of doublet and hose. Where do you go? Leicester Square is still literally a green field site and Soho still had huntsmen riding across it (it is still of course a hunting ground but for other sorts of excitement). You would take a stroll over London Bridge and walk through what was once the entertainment centre for City-folk, a place where some of Shakespeare's immortal lines were first heard (and where immediately afterwards the stage might be given over to rather more barbaric diversions.) This is Southwark and Bankside, where a Bishop once profited out of whorehouses and a cathedral nestles happily next to a prison and a brewery. Naturally everyone we meet on other walks will accompany us – Dr Johnson, Samuel Pepys, Christopher Wren and of course The Bard of Avon (which sounds so much more romantic than the Bard of Bankside!) It was also the place where inns were rather thick on the ground because of its unique position at the southern gateway to the metropolis, with landlords eager to take in weary travellers and lighten the load of their money.

The Walk

We, alas, are merely modern walkers following in their boot prints so we have other hazards to contend with. Bearing this in mind, first come out of London Bridge station, making sure that you are on the right side of the road. If you aren't – don't attempt to cross the oncoming traffic unless you are part kami-kaze hero and part superman – the traffic here works on the principle that 10-stone human versus 10-ton lorry is no contest! So having got yourself out of the correct subway exit you will find yourself going past Southwark Cathedral, which is the earliest Gothic church in London and it is probably one of the few churches in the capital which also have the dubious honour of having housed both a bakery and a pigsty!

Not far down the road in Bermondsey there was an abbey which had an even more convenient purpose; it was somewhere to put redundant queens since both Queen Katherine, (widow to Henry V) and Queen Elizabeth Woodville, (Edward IV's widow and Henry VIII's grandmother) both ended up here somewhat in disgrace in the attached convent. One rather appalling story about the widowed Queen Katherine is that she requested that her body should be left unburied and it remained on display for 200 years in Westminster Abbey merely covered by a loose cloth. Pepys mentions this rather ghoulish tourist attraction when he claims to have "kissed a queen" – but then as we have seen before the diarist was anything but fussy in his choice of female companions!

Having closely inspected the tombs which are in Southwark (including the one commemorating Dr Lockyer who invented a pill which guaranteed immortality – obviously the pill didn't work for its inventor!), turn right out of the Cathedral, down past the Kathleen and May which is an attractive old schooner built at the turn of the century and is open to the public. Here you will go past the Old Thameside Inn, a pleasant enough pub, (in honesty I think the word "old" refers to the Thames rather than the Inn, but don't let that stop you popping in for a drink.

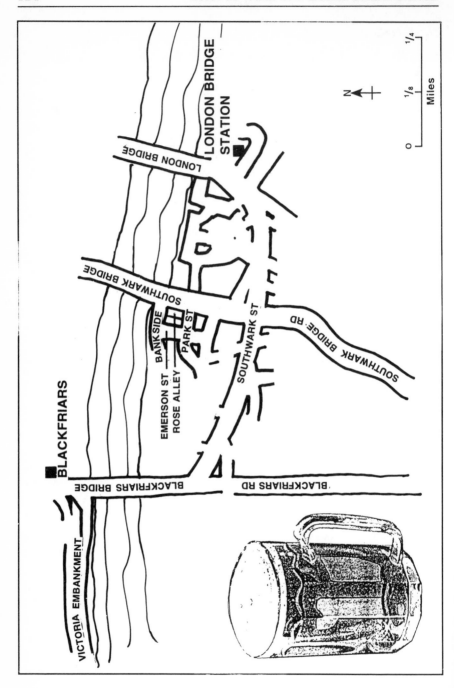

Bishop of Winchester's Palace

You have now come to the Bishop of Winchester's palace. The palace itself witnessed the wedding reception of James I of Scotland and (it is said) the first meeting of Henry VIII and wife number five, Catherine Howard (you may recall she was one of the beheaded ones).

As you can see from the sort of people he used to entertain, the Bishop was an important man, but particularly in these parts since not only was he the main landlord but he also held the responsibility for keeping law and order. The principle industry of the district was what would today be called "vice" and thus the young ladies who worked here were called "Winchester Geese". From as early as 1161 these houses were theoretically, strictly regulated and licensed to carry on their trade. The ulterior motive was naturally the discouragement of "sin" within the City of London (a vain hope) and some of the rules included the limiting of rent for a prostitute's room to 14 pence per week and that no woman who took money from a man to "lie with him" could then leave him until the next morning.

As it happened any man visiting the brothels of Bankside during the day would find it difficult to get back after dark since Thames wherrymen were ordered to moor their craft on the City side at nightfall and the gates to London Bridge were closed at curfew. And swimming through all that raw sewage was out of the question ... ! The arrival of syphilis in England prompted the kind of panic which such things always cause and in 1503 the brothels were officially closed. (Naturally they were all open again a year later). In an act of supreme hypocrisy Henry VIII (not noted for his celibacy – he himself died of syphilis!) closed the official ones again in 1545. They were reopened in 1550 and in order to make sure that there was no confusion they were required to paint their signs on the walls rather than having hanging signs as in the inns and taverns. Which was probably very convenient for those customers who having had their fill in the pub could easily make out where to go for their next entertainment session!

Those people who broke the rules in this part of the world were sent to the "Clink" prison. The prison was used to confine religious prisoners during the frequent changes of faith in the sixteenth century, so it has housed some very devout as well as some very dissolute characters. Not surprisingly the place was also a popular one with rioters, who would release the prisoners (naturally also "despoiling" the brothels – because if you are going to riot you should do things properly). The Gordon rioters took things a little too far in 1780 – they simply burnt the place down.

The Anchor

Hoping they had let the prisoners out first, we will now walk on to pleasanter things and to The Anchor, Bankside, where I am afraid Dr Johnson is waiting for you. This pub (it claims to be the oldest inn site in London) stands on the site of the Castell on the Hoope. It may have been the place where Pepys sat and watched the Great Fire of London and it may well have a network of passages and secret doors leading to the old Clink Prison. As with all the best buildings the stories are legion and very few of them are provable. Anyhow Dr Johnson probably came and drank here (why not – he went everywhere else and this pub was at least owned by his best friend the local brewery owner, Mr Thrale. So even if he couldn't drink for free here, his credit must have been good!) There are a few things which are for sure: it has a splendid beer garden which offers a superb view of the Thames, Southwark Bridge and of course the City of London. It also has plenty of snug nooks and crannies and is full of atmosphere. When you look across the Thames, look back towards Tower Bridge where the top of the Tower of London is just visible.

Rose Theatre

As you turn left out of the Anchor, past the Financial Times newspaper, which let's face is housed in a remarkable building, even if it's not to everybody's taste. Walk up the steps of Southwark bridge having imbibed deeply both of liquid refreshment and the spirit of Dr Johnson (the spirit is probably enough – reading his writings requires rather more stamina) walk past Rose Alley (site of the Rose Theatre where Shakespeare's contemporary Ben Jonson once earned the extraordinarily small sum of 3s. 9d (about 19p) as a playwright. The best seat in the house was about 5p so this gives you some idea of his earnings. It was undoubtedly a small sum even then since he had to borrow £4.00 from his boss on the same day! Ben Jonson was also Shakespeare's friend – which was probably a good thing for Shakespeare since Jonson seems to have had a somewhat fiery temper. He killed one of his colleagues in a fight (fortunately escaping hanging by claiming benefit of clergy – even in 1598 a practically obsolete law that if you could read a verse from the Bible you must be a man of the cloth and therefore could be pardoned a first offence.)

Beer Gardens

Next to Rose Alley is Bear Gardens which commemorates another Elizabethan/Jacobean pastime which is definitely less palatable to us than Hamlet or A Midsummer Night's Dream. Unfortunately, previous inhabitants of this part of the world liked to watch bear baiting (this included Good Queen Bess herself). Samuel Pepys some sixty or seventy years later said he "saw some good sport of the bulls tossing the dogs – one into the very boxes"; he then redeems himself a little by adding "but it is a very rude and nasty pleasure." Ben Jonson in his play Bartholomew Fair talks about the sweeping up after the bears before the performance of the play – they were not so fussy about separating high art and popular performance in those days.

But for all that they were a rough lot then and Pepys also reports watching a "prize fight" take place in one of the ale houses by the Bear Gardens where a butcher and a waterman were in competition and were pretty soon joined by their fellow butchers and watermen in a general free-for-all. Pepys, quite sensibly disappeared as soon as he could, fearing "in the tumult" that he "might get some hurt"!

This is unlikely to happen to us these days, so take a quiet stroll along here, sometimes watching people unaccountably looking for things in the mud. I dread to think what they might find – although it is unlikely to be dead bodies, which used to be fished up quite regularly on these banks.

At this point take a moment to pause and ponder on this side of the river which is so quiet that you can actually hear the traffic from the other side. Down Bear Gardens (don't worry it's quite respectable now) and then you can walk past the site of the Anchor Brewery which was owned by the Thrales in the late eighteenth century. Yes, Dr Johnson now pokes his ungainly head in again. As we have seen, Johnson was very best friends with the Thrales (particularly – and platonically – Mrs Thrale) until as a widow she remarried to someone he didn't like. I feel we must give Johnson some credit for being a canny chap when he described the brewery as not merely "a parcel of boilers and vats, but the potentiality of growing rich beyond the dreams of avarice". Perhaps it was Johnson's tragedy to have been born a man of exceedingly boring eighteenth-century letters – his vocation was obviously twentieth-century marketing! The tradition of brewing in Southwark reaches back a long way. There is a little rhyme which begins:

The nappy strong ale of Southwirke . . .

The tradition is kept up today in a tiny brewery which recently opened at 2 Park Street called Bishops Brewery – we can only hope that they realise Johnson's dream of riches!

Shakespeare's Globe

Now we've walked back to Southwark Bridge – along Bankside again and now you can see Shakespeare's Globe or rather the reconstruction thereof. As this book is being written, the theatre is within a year or so of completion. It is the dream of the late Sam Wanamaker who as a young man came to London and was appalled to see that there was no real monument to the man who was arguably the world's greatest (or certainly most popular and probably most misquoted) poet and playwright.

Shakespeare's own Globe was in what is now Park Street and came to a rather sticky (or rather fiery) end. During a somewhat too dazzling performance of the Bard's Henry VIII (considering the play's history of pyrotechnics it is perhaps not surprising that it is rarely performed these days) in 1613 a stray cannon shot, set fire to the thatched roof and soon the whole building had burnt down. The story goes that actors and audience escaped unhurt except for one

unfortunate spectator whose burning trousers had to be put out by a quick-thinking companion with a bottle of ale (brewed in South-wark perhaps?). More importantly for posterity (but no doubt to the bitter regret of numberless schoolchildren since) Shakespeare's scripts were saved. The theatre was rebuilt but it was doomed and where the fire failed the Puritans succeeded and closed the Globe forever in 1642.

Bankside Jetty

We are now on Bankside Jetty where you can sit down and have a rest after reading about the excitement of the original Globe's disappearance. If you have a burning (!) desire to know about Shakespearean London visit the Shakespeare Exhibition and donate a little more money to finish the new Globe (fire regulations will be strictly adhered to this time!) .

Back at the Bankside Jetty look around at this extraordinary little bit of London. The little row of buildings occupies Cardinal's Wharf which was very likely named after Cardinal Wolsey, who was so intimately involved in trying to get Henry VIII divorced from his first wife Katharine of Aragon when the faithless King fell in love with Anne Boleyn. The episode ended up in the establishment of the Church of England. Ironically enough, Katharine herself was supposed to have first set foot on English soil here when she came as a young princess from Spain to marry Henry's elder brother (unfortunately he died before they could tie the knot, so Katharine was handed down the line to the next heir to the throne – modern English newspapers would have had a field day on that piece of scandal!) Of course, if she'd known what trouble the whole business was going to cause she probably would have refused to get off the boat!

Nestling in the little row of buildings behind you is the house Christopher Wren is supposed to have lived in while he built St Paul's Cathedral on the opposite side of the river. However, this building looks so wobbly that Wren himself could never have built it – or he had a jolly good builder to sort out his plans across the

Thames! There is also a little alley which doesn't lead anywhere called Cardinal Cap Alley. In earlier days visitors may well have not been bothered by its dead-end appearance since it might have housed the Cardinal's Hat brothel. If it did, and the establishment carried such an ecclesiastical name it is rather a sad fact that the women who earned their living there (along with all the other prostitutes in the area) were not permitted a Christian burial but were thrown into unconsecrated ground up the road in Redcross Street (probably near Redcross Way off Southwark Street).

It is probably time to have a moment of spiritual cleansing now, so stand in front of Bankside power station and look across the river where you can see so many church spires. As we have remarked before it is so peaceful here that the traffic sounds quite distant on the other side of the river.

Blackfriars Bridge

Keep on walking past The Founders Arms which is not a prepossessing pub but has superb views of the river. You are still walking along the Thames Path looking towards the City on the right. You are now passing under a railway bridge and then follow the signs to walk up the steps to Blackfriars bridge itself. Although this particular bridge was built in the last century it replaced one which had been funded out of the fines imposed on people who had refused to take on the duties of Sheriff of the City of London. Is this the way forward for public sector funding? No doubt the Treasury have already thought of it!

Up on Blackfriars Bridge, you will pass back under the care of the griffins of the City of London. For a drink before taking the train home at Blackfriars station, you might care to go into Doggetts Coat and Badge, a huge pub with several bars on many floors and a very good restaurant with some of the best views of the City of London. Probably more interesting than this modern pub's architecture is the race it is named after. Doggett's Coat and Badge is a rowing race founded in 1714 by Thomas Doggett, a renowned actor-manager and organised by the Fishmongers Company. The Coat itself is orange with a silver badge and is competed for every summer over a four and a half mile course. It is apparently the oldest regular sporting event in the country.

The Black Friar

Out of the Doggett's Coat and Badge and over the bridge, you will come to Blackfriars Station. Before you go home, another pub which must be visited is the Black Friar, which was remodelled in 1905 in the Arts and Crafts style. But it really isn't necessary to have much appreciation of art movements to stand in awe of this pub. The outside looks fairly unprepossessing and the only clue to its extraordinary interior is a carved friar. Inside it is a riot of marble with nursery rhymes, monks, hide-aways and a beautiful brass bar all crammed inside what is really not a very big pub. The fact that the original licensee bankrupted himself through this extravaganza is not surprising!

If there is only time to visit one pub on this walk, this is the one to go to. The fact that it is at the finish is a bonus – it means that you can spend as much time as you like in there!

15. Strolling down Fleet Street

Highlights: The Royal Air Force Church, where Dr Johnson had a private pew. Fleet Street and the Wig and Pen club. Ye (unmissable) Olde Cheshire Cheese and the pub where Pocahontas was a guest of the Savages.

Stations: Temple and St Pauls

Distance: 1 mile

The Walk

Come out of Temple Station and walk up Arundel Street until you come to St Clement Danes, the Royal Air Force Church. There are a few other interesting points about this Church before we go any further including the fact that Dr Johnson was a regular visitor and had his own pew near to the pulpit. I have to admit that the people buried in the Church come into the category of "friends of" rather than household names in themselves (John Donne's wife, Ben Jonson's best friend etc.) but for sports fans it can boast a real star as one of the rectors – the man who first picked up the ball and ran with it! Yes, William Webb-Ellis, after inventing rugby settled down here and became a man of the cloth.

Essex Street

While wondering in which of the many pubs around here he may have rendered the first rugby songs, we shall take a small diversion down Essex Street. We are going to visit a couple of pubs which have histories which belie their modest outward appearances. The Edgar Wallace, for instance, was renamed after the crime writer (who was,

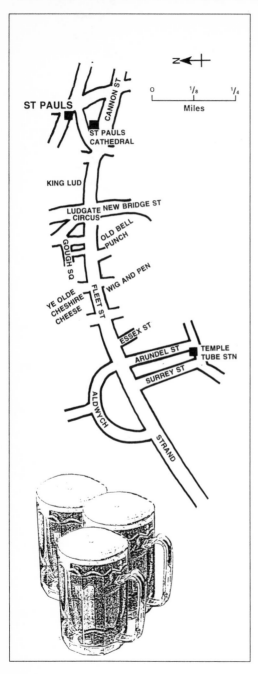

by the way a teetollar) in 1975. It is a Victorian building but stands on the site of The Essex Head, an ancient tavern which played host to Sam's Club, yet another one of Dr Johnson's regular haunts. The club was named after Sam Greaves, the landlord, a former servant of Dr Johnson's friends the Thrales. Dr Johnson used to grace the place with his presence three times a week. It also marks the spot where The Young Pretender, Bonnie Prince Charlie stayed secretly in London.

We can only imagine the building which was once there, but a little further round the corner is Devereux Court (named after Robert Devereux, Earl of Essex who once lived here). This place has a sad history of blood and violence. Here is the Devereux Arms, formerly known as The Grecian Coffee House. In its day (and before it was "refurbished" in the nineteenth century) this splendid pub played host to the cleverest men in the kingdom such as Isaac Newton and Dr Halley (of Halley's Comet fame). The Royal Society and The Royal Academy used to dine here, and occasionally even the Privy Council were known to pop in. But it wasn't all elegant conversation and timeless wit. These days academics confine their arguments to heated exchanges in learned journals, but the ivory towers of scholarship in the eighteenth century obviously also required artillery-proof walls – discussions then took a more assertive note. There is a story that two gentleman scholars actually got so incensed over how to write a particular Greek word that they ended up duelling to the death outside the pub. But they lived in violent times and danger was obviously never far away from this apparently sedate institution. On another occasion a barrister narrowly escaped death from bullets fired into the coffee house. History does not record whether this was another spelling query or merely a psychopath on the loose.

Old Mitre Court

Having been careful not to say anything academically contentious, walk back to the Strand and with the magnificent Royal Courts of Justice on the left-hand side, pause a moment by Old Mitre Court, the second site of The Mitre Inn, where Dr Johnson,(who knew a good pub when he saw one) said "if a young fellow led in a wench (here) both parties at least had to be well dressed." Other places of course were not so fussy, and Boswell (who definitely wasn't fussy) complains that after he had taken "a monstrous big whore" to a tavern offered her a price which obviously was not acceptable (he charmingly comments "her avarice was as big as her a——.") But he goes on to comment on the rascality of the waiters in these infamous sort of taverns. "They connive with the whores, and do what they can to fleece the gentlemen". Before the Inn moved slightly Eastwards to its final resting place in the Court itself, Shakespeare was rumoured to have written there. Of course the whole lot disappeared in 1829 to make room for a bank, so not a lot changes does it!

Fleet Street

On to more salubrious drinkers. We are now walking past the Wig and Pen Club one half of which is housed in a building dating from 1625 which miraculously escaped the Great Fire.The Club (as you can tell by the name) was originally intended for writers and lawyers, but these days will accept anybody.

Of course, we are now in Fleet Street, once home to the English newspaper industry (now, like the lost tribes of Israel scattered diaspora-like all over London but mostly to the Promised Land of Docklands).

Appropriately enough, as you would expect in the street of a thousand journalists, access to alcohol is anything but restricted. The famous pubs here are legion or rather it would be truer to say were legion. Taverns which welcomed the likes of Pepys, Ben Jonson (and of course Samuel Johnson) have been swept away by development and progress. On the other hand, remember the rumour that Tips (an acronym apparently for To Insure Prompt Service) started in Fleet Street Taverns (although I can't believe it hadn't been thought of before!) But we should be grateful that some of the most interesting are left. For instance, on the opposite side of the street to the Wig and Pen Club, there is that most famous of London pubs, Ye Olde Cheshire Cheese.

Ye Olde Cheshire Cheese

Avoid this pub at your peril – if you are merely visiting London, everyone back home will expect you to have been there. If you are not a tourist, why haven't you been there already? Every writer of any note seems to have drunk here at some time – the list is endless: everyone from Dickens to Mark Twain, Tennyson to Conan Doyle. Ben Jonson the Jacobean poet and playwright was even engaged in a poetry competition there. His opponent came up with:

I, Sylvester
Kiss'd your sister

the rejoinder came

I Ben Jonson
Kiss'd your wife.

"it doesn't rhyme" said Sylvester; "No, but it's true" said Jonson. Perhaps not worthy of a Poet Laureate (as Jonson was) but it was unlikely that anyone would argue with him since he had previously murdered one argumentative colleague in a tavern brawl!

What seems strange is that despite the fact that Dr Johnson lived right on top of the pub in Gough Square (and had been heard to remark that a chair in a tavern was "the throne of human felicity") there is no documentary evidence to prove that he used to come and drink here. People are reported to have remembered seeing him there, but nobody wrote it down! However, even without absolute proof that Dr Johnson "was here" (in fact he is reported as saying that after he moved over the road to this side of Fleet Street "nothing but a hurricane" would have induced him to cross back again). He was reported as having been seen there with his friends by a very old customer some fifty years later. Dr Johnson had an impressive intellect – but he also made an impression physically. One contemporary remembers his progress as "heavily headlong". Remember that Fleet Street in Johnson's day was not the wide boulevard it is now and had no pedestrian pavements, so if Johnson met with an obstacle such as a porter laden with baggage, the outcome was inevitable – Johnson would simply walk through the poor man, scattering him and his load on the cobbles. It is recorded as one of the few occasions that a London porter was left speechless (although no doubt silently contemplating words which were definitely not contained in the famous Dictionary!)

Wine Office Court

Beween Gough Square (where Johnson wrote the Dictionary) and Ye Olde Cheshire Cheese is Wine Office Court where licences for selling wine were once issued. Oliver Goldsmith (author of that mainstay of amateur theatricals – She Stoops to Conquer) also lived and wrote The Vicar of Wakefield here. Can we spare a thought for poor old Oliver in passing? Despite writing such charming books and (when he had the money) being gloriously generous, he was over-sensitive, cursed with the most appalling dress sense and ugly to boot. It couldn't have been fun being Goldsmith, so perhaps he drowned his sorrows at the Cheese? Although apparently as he was permanently poverty-stricken perhaps he had to wait until Johnson bought him a pint? It is said that Johnson, who was one of Goldsmith's greatest friends, actually took the manuscript of the Vicar of Wakefield around to the publisher and sold it for sixty guineas to save his chum from the bailiffs.

David Garrick, the actor, wrote Goldmith's epitaph for his monument in Westminster Abbey:

"Here lies poor Nolly Goldsmith, for shortness called Noll,
Who wrote like an angel but talked like poor Poll."

Whether or not Johnson or Goldsmith drank in the Cheese, the pub has enough more recent stories to keep you interested. There were the huge puddings which they used to make, which took 16 hours to cook, could weigh up to 80lb and could serve up to 90 people. There was even a parrot not surprisingly called Polly who had been left as an unsolicited gift by a passing seaman. This creature, although foul-mouthed could do a passable imitation of a wine bottle being corked and was so renowned that when she died in 1926, the sad event was reported in 200 newspapers around the world (no doubt because the London reporters of all those newspapers just "happened" to be in the pub at the time!)

El Vinos

A more recent drinking spot, El Vino's, witnessed a real revolution in the 1960s when it refused to serve women at the bar (because of the "clutter" of handbags etc. – this was before the advent of mobile phones remember) and the management decreed they had to be served at tables.The long running saga became known as The Battle of Fleet Street. It was finally decided in 1982 in favour of the women. One can only assume that it went on so long because journalists could not let a good story in a local pub die!

The Cock Tavern

As you stroll further down Fleet Street, on the other side to the Cheese, you will come upon the Cock Tavern, which is another pub which is in a different place to where it started out. It had originally been on the other side of the road where it had apparently been established in 1549. The present building dates from 1887. As you would expect this was another favourite of writers, from Pepys (who it must be admitted was probably more interested in the women he brought there than the excellent chops, steaks and porters.) One can only assume that Dickens, Thackeray and Tennyson were rather less lascivious in their pursuits at the Cock. It must have been a pretty cheerful place to make Tennyson (otherwise better known for the

far less amusing Charge of the Light Brigade, and the Lady of
Shallott) wrote a monologue which went

> *O plump head-waiter at the Cock*
> *To which I most resort*
> *How goes the time 'Tis five o'clock.*
> *Go fetch a pint of port."*

The quality of the poet laureate's verse did not go unappreciated –
apparently when the original pub was demolished, Tennyson was
sent a piece of it as a memento. The Cock which stands in the bar
(reputedly by Grinling Gibbons) and the sideboard are all that is left
of the pub now.

Further down Fleet Street we come to two pubs which are still in
the place in which they were first put, the Punch Tavern and the
Old Bell although neither of them seem to have managed to keep the
names they were born with.

The Old Bell

First the Old Bell. The pub, which has rejoiced in the names Golden
Bell and the Twelve Bells possibly stands on the site of the workshop
of Wynken de Worde (in turn on the site of another inn called The
Swan) – an ideal location for a printer and bookseller, nicely posi-
tioned between the seat of government at Westminster and the
corridors of commerce, with lots of literate passing trade. Some
writers claim the pub was built by Sir Christopher Wren to enable
his workmen to have a drink while building St Bride's Church which
had been destroyed in the Great Fire. Naturally other writers claim
that it is simply the same age as St Bride's but whatever the case it
is certainly a charming little place. St Bride's elegant spire has been
the model for countless wedding cakes since it was built in the late
seventeenth century – that fact has nothing to do with the pub, but
I thought I would throw it in case you thought I had forgotten!

Punch Tavern

Nearly next door to the Old Bell is the Punch Tavern. Contrary to
popular belief, this tavern is not where the magazine of the same

name first started. The Edinburgh Castle in the Strand (now disappeared) had that honour – however, so many of the staff of that fine magazine used to hang about in the Crown and Sugar Loaf in Fleet Street, that eventually they changed the name of the pub! Alas, it is now a pub without the magazine – but you can drink to its memory in the pub surrounded by mementoes.

Pocahontas at the Belle Sauvage

Suitably saddened by the loss of this fine publication you must (carefully) cross New Bridge Street straight ahead of you and look over the road at the King Lud which is about all that is left of the multitude of inns which would greet the pilgrim or traveller on their way to the City of London or St Pauls Cathedral. I have to admit that this tavern is not over exciting but if you shut your eyes you may be able to imagine the Belle Sauvage Yard which stood next to it. This was a real King among pubs. Pocahontas stayed here in 1617 and the Savages (the then owners of the pub) hung a picture of her on their wall – and so they say this long vanished pub earned its name as the Belle Sauvage.

It has to be said that she may not have been very comfortable while she stayed there. In the eighteenth century one Parson Woodforde, (who has now had a brewery named after him), commented on the place "I was bit terribly by the bugs last night but it did not wake me" but sad to say four years later he commented "I was bit so terribly with bugs again this night that I got up at 4 o'clock this morning and took a long walk". Still later he reported "I did not take off my clothes . . . but set up in a Great Chair all night with my Feet on the Bed and slept very well considering and not pestered with bugs". At least there has been some progress in the hotel trade since then because Parson Woodforde also declared what "a very good house it is". Good grief – what were the bad ones like!

More comfortingly, the King Lud was well known from 1864 to 1875 for its gargantuan portions of Welsh Rarebit.

On the last gasps of the walk now, so let us stroll along towards St Pauls looking up at Queen Anne as we pass her statue and reflect on the doggerel:

Brandy Nan, Brandy Nan, left in the lurch,
Your face to the Gin Shop, your back to the Church.

It's a shame you can't peek under the skirts of the statue. Have you
never wondered what genuine Queen Anne legs really looked like?
Were they sturdy and bow-legged and did she, as some sort of early
form of callisthenics often carry balls in her feet? This is just one of
those questions which serious historians refuse to answer.

As you walk past St Pauls, here are a few facts which have been
recorded which you might find worth considering. The St Paul's
before the one we know now (there have been five in all) was used
more or less as a street, with horses and donkeys being led up the
nave, and stalls set up on the tombs on either side. Religious services
of course never got in the way of trade and presumably during a
particularly dry sermon you could pick up a drink or two and a bite
of something sustaining. Since sermons could easily last a few
hours, this could have been quite as necessary as an ice cream at the
cinema or the coffee in the interval.

When the Great Fire destroyed St Pauls, the unfortunate Sir
Christopher Wren had three different attempts at pleasing the various bodies who had to approve the building. He took his work
seriously and burst into tears when the second plan was rejected.
You may well ask why he bothered at all since it was 41 years before
the authorities paid him in full. Not surprisingly the building of St
Pauls, which took 28 years to complete became a by-word for the
proverbial slowness of builders. As everyone knows, they haven't
got any faster – but what excuses did they use then? "My horse/don-
key/ass/handcart broke down" or "I just had to finish the church/pal-
ace/mansion up the road?" or "Had a touch of plague this morning"?
But even more intriguingly, did builders reveal tantalising inches of
midriff bulge in those days? Or is this phenomenon brought about
by excess lager and jeans? The historian who discovers this will be
a hero/heroine indeed.

Perhaps we will never know – but here is St Pauls Tube. Ponder
these intriguing questions on the way home!

More Sigma Books – in & around London

RAILWAY RAMBLES: London & the South-East
Clive Higgs

Here is an excellent collection of walks all accesible by London's railways. They are within a 50-mile radius of London and range from three to seven miles. Clive even tells you what can be seen 'from the carriage window' on your way to the walks.

£4.95

LONDON BUS-TOP TOURIST
John Wittich

See London from the top of a London bus - hop off and visit an attraction - then carry on to see the sights that everybody just has to see, and many places that the tourists rarely visit. Written by a well-known guide and lecturer registered with the London Tourist Board.

£6.95

TEA SHOP WALKS IN THE CHILTERNS
Jean Patefield

Scones with strawberry jam, home-made cakes, toasted tea-cakes. What could be better than to enjoy a country walk and a typical English afternoon tea! Walks from two to seven . miles with plenty of information to add pleasure to the walks.

£6.95

BY-WAY BIKING IN THE CHILTERNS
Henry Tindell

650 square miles to tackle with your bike! Here are 22 circular routes from 7 to 20 miles, plus a return route on the Oxfordshire Cycleway for a total of over 50 miles. The routes are on quiet country roads and bridleways suitable for almost every sort of cyclist.

£7.95

Country Walking in England & Wales:

THE LAKELAND SUMMITS – Tim Synge *(£7.95)*

100 LAKE DISTRICT HILL WALKS – Gordon Brown *(£7.95)*

LAKELAND ROCKY RAMBLES: Geology beneath your feet – Brian Lynas *(£7.95)*

FULL DAYS ON THE FELLS: Challenging Walks – Adrian Dixon *(£7.95)*

PUB WALKS IN THE LAKE DISTRICT – Neil Coates *(£6.95)*

LAKELAND WALKING, ON THE LEVEL – Norman Buckley *(£6.95)*

MOSTLY DOWNHILL: LEISURELY WALKS, LAKE DISTRICT – Alan Pears *(£6.95)*

WALKS IN MYSTERIOUS WALES – Laurence Main *(£7.95)*

TEA SHOP WALKS IN CHESHIRE – Clive Price *(£6.95)*

TEA SHOP WALKS IN THE LAKE DISTRICT – Jean Patefield *(£6.95)*

TEA SHOP WALKS IN THE CHILTERNS – Jean Patefield *(£6.95)*

MOSTLY DOWNHILL IN THE PEAK DISTRICT – Clive Price *(£6.95)*
(two volumes, White Peak & Dark Peak)

EAST CHESHIRE WALKS – Graham Beech *(£5.95)*

WEST CHESHIRE WALKS – Jen Darling *(£5.95)*

HILL WALKS IN MID WALES – Dave Ing *(£8.95)*

WELSH WALKS: Dolgellau /Cambrian Coast – L. Main & M. Perrott *(£5.95)*

WELSH WALKS: Aberystwyth & District – L. Main & M. Perrott *(£5.95)*

RAMBLES IN NORTH WALES – Roger Redfern *(£6.95)*

PUB WALKS IN SNOWDONIA – Laurence Main *(£6.95)*

BEST PUB WALKS IN GWENT – Les Lumsdon *(£6.95)*

PUB WALKS IN POWYS – Les Lumsdon & Chris Rushton *(£6.95)*

BEST PUB WALKS IN PEMBROKESHIRE – Laurence Main *(£6.95)*

RAMBLES AROUND MANCHESTER – Mike Cresswell *(£5.95)*

LAKELAND WALKING: On The Level – Norman Buckley *(£6.95)*

FIFTY CLASSIC WALKS IN THE PENNINES – Terry Marsh *(£8.95)*

WEST PENNINE WALKS – Mike Cresswell *(£5.95)*

BEST PUB WALKS IN ESSEX – Derek Keeble *(£6.95)*

More Pub Walks . . .

There are many more titles in our fabulous series of 'Pub Walks' books for just about every popular walking area in the UK, all featuring access by public transport. We label our more recent ones as 'best' to differentiate them from inferior competitors!

Cycling . . .

CYCLE UK! The essential guide to leisure cycling – Les Lumsdon *(£9.95)*

OFF-BEAT CYCLING IN THE PEAK DISTRICT – Clive Smith *(£6.95)*

MORE OFF-BEAT CYCLING IN THE PEAK DISTRICT – Clive Smith *(£6.95)*

50 BEST CYCLE RIDES IN CHESHIRE – edited by Graham Beech *(£7.95)*

CYCLING IN THE COTSWOLDS – Stephen Hill *(£6.95)*

CYCLING IN THE LAKE DISTRICT – John Wood *(£7.95)*

CYCLING IN LINCOLNSHIRE – Penny & Bill Howe *(£7.95)*

CYCLING IN STAFFORDSHIRE – Linda Wain *(£7.95)*

CYCLING IN THE WEST COUNTRY – Helen Stephenson *(£7.95)*

CYCLING IN SOUTH WALES – Rosemary Evans *(£7.95)*

CYCLING IN SCOTLAND & N.E.ENGLAND – Philip Routledge *(£7.95)* .

CYCLING IN NORTH WALES – Philip Routledge *(£7.95) ... available 1996*

BY-WAY BIKING IN THE CHILTERNS – Henry Tindell *(£7.95)*

Sport . . .

RED FEVER: from Rochdale to Rio as 'United' supporters – Steve Donoghue *(£7.95)*

UNITED WE STOOD: unofficial history of the Ferguson years – Richard Kurt *(£6.95)*

MANCHESTER CITY: Moments to Remember – John Creighton *(£9.95)*

- plus many more entertaining and educational books being regularly added to our list. All of our books are available from your local bookshop. In case of difficulty, or to obtain our complete catalogue, please contact:

Sigma Leisure, 1 South Oak Lane, Wilmslow, Cheshire SK9 6AR
Phone: 01625 – 531035   Fax: 01625 – 536800

ACCESS and VISA orders welcome – call our friendly sales staff or use our 24 hour Answerphone service! Most orders are despatched on the day we receive your order – you could be enjoying our books in just a couple of days. Please add £2 p&p to all orders.